OUT OF MY DEPTHS

BOOKS BY PAUL WEST

The Very Rich Hours of Count von Stauffenberg
Gala
Bela Lugosi's White Christmas
Colonel Mint
Caliban's Filibuster
Words for a Deaf Daughter
I'm Expecting to Live Quite Soon
Tenement of Clay
Alley Jaggers
The Wine of Absurdity
I, Said the Sparrow
The Snow Leopard
Byron and the Spoiler's Art

OUT OF MY DEPTHS

A Swimmer in the Universe

Paul West

Anchor Press/Doubleday
Garden City, New York
1983

This Anchor Press edition is the first publication of
OUT OF MY DEPTHS
Anchor Press: 1983

Library of Congress Cataloging in Publication Data

West, Paul, 1930–
Out of my depths.

1. Swimming—Psychological aspects.
2. Swimming—Philosophy.
I. Title.
GV838.53.P75W47   1983   797.2'1'01
ISBN: 0-385-18083-7
Library of Congress Catalog Card Number: 82–9722

First Edition

For Diane Ackerman:
poet of the planets and the cosmic overwhelm,
pilot, equestrian, scholar,
and my long-suffering swim tutor:
these amoretti *of a veteran beginner,*
with love and gratitude

CONTENTS

What would depth be without lighting?

MARTIN HEIDEGGER,
Remembrance of the Poet

OUT OF MY DEPTHS

1. SEA FEVER

. . . to myself I seem to have been only like a boy playing on the sea-shore, and diverting myself in now and
then finding a smoother pebble or a prettier shell than
ordinary, while the great ocean of truth lay all undis-
covered before me.

SIR ISAAC NEWTON,
a short time before his death

Shrines invite the gods but often go empty. And, when most of your life you try for something less grand, such as learning to swim, and flunk it, you feel emptier than any shrine, older than water itself, dumber than the mindless hydrogen that builds a helium star. Between boyhood and halfway to ninety, I floundered embarrassed among toddlers in the shallows of pools, always heading back from the line that read four feet six inches but meant certain death to me. Only with both hands gripping the angle or curb of the slop channel did I let my legs come up for interludes of levitation, when another planet cruising by seemed to pull with bigger gravity. When my legs wafted up, I should have *known* that swimming worked, that I too was allowed it; but I couldn't bring myself to try that much abandon.

Once, in four feet, as my legs came up and I for once was facing down, an oldish man swam underwater clean beneath them, having swum that way from the deep end and continuing until his fingers grazed the wading steps: an invader, I thought, a reptilian undertow, come and gone as an oblique flash in an elongated reach past me and my stranded legs. How I envied him his water-easiness when he left under my shin fronts only the fizz of his going, which when a ship's propellers make it is called cavitation, from the brief cavity torn in the water. It felt, after he'd gone, like a concertina series of those trees made from newspapers. The bubbles tickled, saying come and play. I swung from my mooring; I felt almost ready to throw up; I let go with one hand, then with the other, yearning for a third, and swayed like a barrel that slowly righted itself as my legs went down and I knew the experiment was over. The water had let me down, whereas I thought I'd almost

conned it that I felt serene. I scrambled out and, coughing
the sob of frustration, gave myself an epic dry, weary after
fifty imaginary laps, even as the man who could swim
plunged in again, now with goggles on, so as to see me thor-
oughly when he made his next foray. He knew a dud when
he saw one, he who had seen countless wrecked steamers
close-up, on the bottom, through his oval visor, and out-
stared barracudas, bumped heads with dolphin and por-
poise, stroked the big blunt whale above its eye, and tugged
at the remoras riding suck on a shark. Yes, he was going to
inspect me as if I were an exhibit behind glass, and dine out
on the story for weeks: of how he'd seen a well-built
landlubber edging in and out, bobbing up and down, anchored to the slop channel like a dead fish being towed har-
borward to be weighed. So far as he was concerned, I
couldn't count or read and wasn't much good at walking either. Even at rest in his coffin, he'd be a niftier swimmer
than I, with crossed hands stroking himself to a better place
in the ground than I would ever find in all the oceans in the
world. And so I tried again, with mind shut off, and headed
for one of my new-found stamping grounds.

In midsummer the shallows off Florida's east coast are
warm as new-breathed air, and your feet, instead of flinching stiff, smooth out like green bananas. You can saunter for
miles along those even beaches, sloshing warm and boneless
with good-tempered pipefish cruising after you, or alongside, glad of a paddler for company, sometimes even touching noses with your feet. And, all around you, plankton you
cannot see, which you know is gorse-yellow or a see-through
white like scratched celluloid, dawdles in the swell of your
transit: a million tiny boomerangs at anchor.

A wading paradise open to all, and mulled by the Gulf
Stream, this was the centerpiece of my euphoria, a shoreline
so tonic it made a child of me in seconds. Down flops a foot

on the sand, and nothing else is real, not the dead jellyfish
that wash up with each tide like tiny bulbous jet planes cut
from soapstone or plastic, not even the cars which on certain accursed days churn the beach into a Beelzebub's or-
chard.

Those cars used to remind me of myself; I, like them, was
a water illiterate. Or *was* I still? Out I waded, then leaned
forward until I overbalanced into four feet of water and
began to lash the surface in a frenzy with both arms, barely
moving ahead but at least telling the sea I was there, a
tilted frothmaker almost prone on its lap. And then, of
course, almost laughing aloud at the notion that I was going
down, going down, I stood again, cursed, repeated the
whole thing and went nosing south, breath not held, and
recovered by wallowing sideways until a leg touched, when
with scalded eyes and putrid mouth I came upright again,
reeling and gasping, aware that I was safe, yet knowing the
panic of someone far beyond the reef or out a long way
from the other coast, deep in the Gulf beyond the buoys.

To recover gracefully from that astonished, wheezing pos-
ture, among blithe horizontal children who kept going
under, I pretended I was Gulliver (whose book begins on
the day after April Fool's), newly freed of his bonds and
rearing up again, dizzy, blurred, and sore. Oh the shame.
No good to kneel, making believe I was wholly immersed
for the crawl, or to squat, as if for the backstroke; down
below, nothing was flat. The only recovery was to blunder
back to the shingle, with eyes fixed on the top floor of a
beach hotel as if expecting or even receiving a summons by
semaphore, one hand canted in a skewed salute that really
masked two bloodshot eyes. Then, after a perfunctory wave
at the semaphorist, I squatted and leaned back where the
wave-slop ran into the sand, and scanned the horizon like a
man from Lloyds in the nineteenth century. Defeated again
and wondering what to do next time (wade into deep water

and trust to luck?), I scooped up handfuls of sand and slung them vengefully into the tide, working my will on at least a cubic foot of it; the rest of it could go hang, or drown, or dry up, just so long as I swam in my little plot of ocean.

My legs, I'd been told by exasperated friends, always hung too low; I must float them up. But they wouldn't budge unless I was holding onto something, and like trailing anchors they took me down. Nor could I discover my center of gravity, my own equivalent (vis-à-vis air) of the line that runs along the wing of a plane, roughly a third of the width behind the leading edge. I had no center, it seemed, though I was nothing but gravity. How much the planet wanted me, I thought, not even letting me play truant in the water. I always either went headfirst down, a crippled U-boat, or sank vertical like a stubborn captain going down with his ship, erect on the bridge. I couldn't even float, and years of agitated high-speed thrashing, while incredulous friends looked away, had propelled me maybe four or five yards: about eighteen inches a year. Had I known then that Samuel Beckett's jock of a father had made him dive into the sea, shouting, "Be a brave boy!" while everybody watched, I'd have felt less isolated, but I'd still have wanted to learn to dive.

Without realizing it, I'd begun to associate mentally with outcasts and grotesques, not only out-size Captain Gulliver and one-legged pirates who couldn't swim, but also Boris Vian's limping, bandaged, bleeding figment, the Schmürz, the passive blob upon whom the other characters in the play *The Empire Builders* vent their pique and rage with kicks and shoves. Not quite an Elephant Man, I was close to Beckett's Watt, who walks with a funambulistic stagger, and his Molloy, who at his halest and heartiest "rides" a chainless bike by shoving his crutches backward. What are you doing? ask the police; but Molloy never knows. Show us your papers, they say. He produces bits of toilet paper.

What, then, was *I* doing on the strand? I had no idea, and could only babble defensive runes: *Somewhere an electric chair is waiting*, stolen from Laurel and Hardy, and *There's nothing on the brink of what you think*, stolen from Duke Ellington. I was messing with the South Atlantic. I was wading, flirting, and tramping about in the water just enough for my recollections of it all, a month later, to glow with near-prowess. *I have been bathing in the South Atlantic.* How grand it sounded, and it was almost true, except that it was a marine form of masturbation. I did everything but swim, becoming quite a connoisseur of water temperature, tidal force, the condition of the sand, the habits of crabs and gulls, the exact aroma of the wind, the taste of sea-borne rain.

Ungainly as Bottom, Rumpelstiltskin, and Friar Tuck combined, I had even dicted for the fray, but nothing worked. Surely my skeleton, hollow with all the bone's marrow gone, would have sunk at once. Stoutness, as people politely called what I then suffered from, had nothing to do with it, whereas an almost total lack of coordination did: I, who passed as an athlete on land, a near maestro with big or little balls traveling at speed, had met my match, and all that remained was a philosophical accommodation to the fact. I felt as if a chunk of my brain (part of the used part too) had died. I was a bag of cement. But the cruelest thrust of all came when one of those gullible, insistent identifiers who throng the coasts came up and asked me what "my sign" was, right after watching me flail and choke. Of course, and to the displeasure of my astronomer friends, I *knew*. But to have to answer "Pisces," even in your mind's ear, in the wake of yet another unfishlike performance, was too much. "I've no idea," I said. "Jesus, you sure look like a Pisces to me," my diviner said, resuming his way astounded by yet another astrological ignoramus, and one with a death wish yet. I was finless, gill-less, and far from glabrous, so I wasn't going to be saddled with some zoological calling card. No, I was man the drowner, the non-rebreather, the swim-bladderless two-legged wonder who, when he flew, made wings and who, when he swam, quite rightly fell into the arms of Mae West. *Homo ambulans:* ambulatory without being pedestrian—that was the sign I'd been born under; but water made me not only pedestrian but a dunce as well. I'd get even yet, I swore each time the lure of pastel azure water conned me south to the seascape of a new disgrace. The secret was there to find, built into the nature of things, along with radium and mc^2 and pi.

What miffed me, even more than the sight of able-bodied swimmers swimming, was that of those who trod water. What were they doing? They were *treading water*, which to me was like playing baseball on a cloud. They weren't gliding or floating. They were taking a static stroll in the midst of the medium that let me down, transferring a land-bound act into the very place it didn't belong. I knew they would all disappear from sight, but the bribed or intimidated water held them up. They talked to one another, without the slightest panic lifted an arm to gesture or to bunt a beach ball, and in general behaved as if seated in invisible armchairs, doing it without thinking about it, as liberated from gravity as aerialists, or sailplane pilots lofted on summer thermals. Perhaps they belonged to a secret society that rehearsed the feat in attics and greenhouses so as to look as nonchalant as this. Or they spent hours in the bath bicycling with their legs, or on soft old-fashioned mattresses which had all the givingness of water. Or even on water beds. Everyone I saw could do it, so I expected them to begin to walk on air as well and to summon their lunch to them along invisible routes between their hotels and their mouths. I was almost ready to believe in the Resurrection after witnessing this aquatic version of the Indian rope trick. Were they humans at all? Or changelings from an-

other planet? Silicon-based hominids made of cork? I left
the beach in disgust, rebuked by a commonplace miracle
that was a parody as well. Surely, if you could do such a
thing, you should do it in private only lest you drive a non-
swimmer, a non-floater, a non-treader right out of his mind.

Once I watched a group form a ring, all holding hands,
and their legs were nowhere in sight. Nothing stirred except
their detestable jolly faces, and I felt I'd seen that for which
there was no word: the abominable, the unspeakable which
the Romans called *infandum*. And yes there were children
doing it too, like bread cast upon the waters and emanci-
pated from the order of time and space. The dead sat up.
The unborn came spiraling down, happy and white, like
crows around an invisible Maypole. How could I not do it?
How could I not try again? All I had to do was assume that
blasé look, lean back, and begin to talk. Nature did the
rest. It was a human birthright, after all, the third mode of
swimming, as Colymbetes had called it in 1538.

I sank, cursing those who'd told me that, once I got the
knack, it was easier than swimming, easier than almost anything. A reef grew in my rear end and took me down. Making exactly the same motions as everybody else, I found I
was not of their company but an obsolete life form, a
doomed offshoot not "selected for," as the jargon has it, at
worst not even regarded as a human phenomenon of any
kind, at best like the pleonastic *ne* in French, which hangs
there in the syntax without meaning anything at all. I trod
with an imaginary plastic dumbbell in each hand, as if to
fool the water; but the water heard me coming and was not
deceived. If there truly was a point I balanced at, as friends
and strangers kept on telling me ("It's impossible not to
have one"), it was never there. Down again, I pretended
not to care. The same happened in chlorinated water as in
salty. I couldn't have managed to tread even in mercury or

pitch; but perhaps I might yet learn to drown with extravagant style, the best drowner in years, at least along that golden coast. Twenty, fifty, times I tried, and people actually trod their own bit of water to watch this swimming fool, who was underwater too often ever to hear the good advice they shouted. All I achieved, after getting the water out of my eyes each time, was the right look: one of faintly strained insouciance, as if you've just detected a pipefish in your trunks. Or, if not that, then the rigor of a wholly shut face as the waterline rises at a centimeter per second, and your stiff upper lip goes down for the count once again. Conceivably, I thought, my own way has to be the inverted one: I can tread upside down, with the soles of my feet doing duty for my face, while my head dawdles, a big buoyant bulb beneath me, and my toes breathe freely; but I could no more get upside down than I could stay on top.

Yet I persisted. I humored myself non-stop, eventually developing in private, so as to impose it on all who watched when I hit the beach, what I called the *Titanic* face: stoical, stunned, one of the insignia of grace under pressure, as if all your life you had wanted only to drown, much as a wildebeest wants to be shot, a bull castrated, a turkey cooked. At least my facial muscles were getting a thorough workout, several times a day, and I finally learned how to secrete the porky stare of the breath-held sinker within the blithe I'm-looking-through-you-while-talking-to-you stare of the adept treader. The one expression turned into the other with minimum incongruity; Canute West, going down to the deep six for the umpteenth time, split the wound of his mouth and bared his teeth in the *Titanic* smile. Self-sacrifice had no finer leer; self-disdain no sharper tooth.

Some things, it was clear, would never be mine. But I had a unique opportunity to convert the different modes of drowning into a new swimming style. When I failed to float, I'd invent the passive stroke known as the deathbed sprawl,

too hard for any but the most adroit to learn. When I failed
to tread, I'd come up with—no, I'd go down in history with
—the toilet squat, as if over one of those Italian holes-in-
concrete which arrange the lower colon vertical and make
evacuating that much easier. Pondering other contortions,
rehearsed on seats but maybe usable in water or midair, I
wondered if there was anything to learn from the difference
between North American and European toilets of the fan-
cier kind. Our own have wide-yawning shallow mouths, like
certain gargoyles, and so much water high up that your
leavings land not far beneath you and float there like a silt
of shame, whereas theirs have acutely tapered deep mouths
and deeper throats (like all genuine gargoyles), at the very
bottom of which stands a modicum of water ready to get
things out of sight as fast as possible. We North Americans
tend to splash our nether regions, therefore, which is oddly
unhygienic for a hygiene-crazy continent, while Europeans
sit remarkably high above their filth for a continent never
fetishistic about flies, hand washing, or last week's grease for
cooking in. Is to be close somehow more real, more tolerant?
Is to be far above more hung up, more obsessed? The sounds
are different too, and so are the expectations; a grave,
unblinking study remains to be done by some De Tocque-
ville-of-the-jakes and certainly before any of us leave to in-
habit another planet.

Then I wondered about other postures, less gross but just
as degraded: holds from wrestling, flogging, *tête-bêche* sex.
I remembered the spread-eagled fey leap of the soccer
player who has scored a goal, the self-prizing self-fondling
delirious run back down the field to kisses, hugs, and palms
on the butt. Why, there were hundreds of ways to manage
it. When I failed to swim, I'd improvise the crucifixion
stretch, which gave you maximum dignity, maximum reli-
gious resonance while giving up the ghost, and also tinged
you with Icarus, who flew in much the same spread-eagled

crimp. Like a dolphin I might even manage an inverted dive, up from twenty feet down, a last desperate gesture as I slammed through the surface, caught the rubber ring around my neck, and went back down without even the reward of a dead fish. I might even, before I perished, perfect the art of underwater seeing. Thousands would swim down just to watch me see: "He sees like nobody's business. Have you ever seen him see? All of his swimming ability's concentrated into his eyes. He's already seen Jesus, Columbus, and Harriet Beecher Stowe." A winch would bring me back to life. An eye bath full of boric acid would restore my sight, and then I'd descend again to report to the underwater world from A to Z.

Such was my way of being aghast. How everyday the secret felt, like sliced bread an Old World milkman caches on the doorstep, hard against the upright, during rain, and firm and dry in its waxen wrapper until someone takes it in, devours it, takes heart from it, then flushes it away underground into living memory. I thought of all the sliced bread that arrived enclosed and went away unseen, famous loaves like Hovis and such rare ones as the almost unfindable manna called Turog. I felt locked out again, from all the privacies in the world; untouched by sign and countersign, challenge and password, even the masonic signs the convicted well-to-do have made from the dock to the unrelenting judge who told them they'd be hanged by the neck until dead. Boy Scout handshakes passed me by. There was no badge behind the lapel of my coat. In what, I wondered, did the secret consist? Was the ability to tread or float (I'd no longer ask to swim if once admitted) unique to a certain pressure in the blood? Or to a certain timbre of the voice or texture of the skin? Was it only the small-handed, short-armed, big-headed, big-assed ones who hit the water wrong? Or those who couldn't do it were the ones the water *didn't want*. There were singularities in physics, when the usual laws went by the board, of which I now had met a live example, not far from what Thomas De Quincey, in one of the most awkward yet most seminal sentences in English called "a compound experience incapable of being disentangled," more fully explained, in *The Affliction of Childhood*, between images of death-in-summer and "long dark evenings" in the firelit nursery, as follows:

> Far more of our deepest thoughts and feelings pass to us through perplexed combinations of concrete objects, pass to us as *involutes* (if I may coin that word) in compound experiences incapable of being disentangled, than ever reach us *directly*, and in their own abstract shapes.

Brooding on De Quincey's diagnostic teaser, in successive fits of helplessness, I soon had the equivalent of a coat of arms for what couldn't be understood even though it had to be endured. Life had to be deciphered like a cryptogram, as André Breton said. Artaud spoke of a concocted being, "made of wood or cloth, entirely invented, corresponding to nothing, yet disquieting by nature, capable of reintroducing on the stage a little breath of . . . metaphysical fear." And Beckett himself, whom I'd been reading on the beach as if in caustic retort to his hearty father, had come to similar recognitions, first in *Watt*, where we hear of "incidents . . . of great formal brilliance and indeterminable purport," and then in *Molloy*, which tells us that "There are things from time to time, in spite of everything, that impose themselves on the understanding with the force of axioms, for unknown reasons." If René Magritte had ever been rash enough to draw me, as he once drew a pipe, he'd have been obliged to write a caption underneath me, saying *This is not a swimmer*. Why? Because I looked just like a swimmer, as almost anyone does, just as the pipe he said wasn't a pipe looked like one. But it was a *drawing* of a pipe, whose origi-

nal, however, must have been a pipe for real, whereas the
original of me wasn't a swimmer in any sense at all.

What a lot of abstract baggage to lug around because of a
raw, undeniable inability. I was simply one of the handicapped, born unable to swim as others had been born deaf,
blind, armless, hare-lipped, spastic, retarded, with exposed
spines, and perforated hearts. I was kin, as well, to those
who couldn't count or spell or read or stop trembling or get
their food into their stomach. All I had to do was join the
non-swimmer in me to what else was wrong with me, then
lift my head, and compare until I was swamped by relief
that I'd got off so lightly. Only a perfectionist, trapped in an
evolutionary idyll iced with unerring genetics, could expect
so much of himself. The human equation was fairly simple:
on the plus side, a preponderance of favorable chances was
the ground against which the minuses figured, and you just
got on with it, able at best to see yourself, and everyone
else, emblematically, as another ripple in the human cloth,
briefly privileged to do something or nothing—Faust or
Dante's lazy Florentine lute maker, Belacqua; Prometheus,
or the Schmürz. It was almost impossible to leave no trace
at all. Who, after three score years and ten, could claim to
have been nothing but a connoisseur of the skin or his or
her God-given hands, or a connoisseur of the gurgling in the
bowels while peristalsis looped the loop? But you could try
to do it, couldn't you? just tuning in to the sensations of
your body going right, much as my father did on the last
day of his life, grateful for a day of no pain for a change,
and able to round everything off by saying, almost with his
final words, what a difference it had made. He had felt
clean and still, with everything in order and for once not
dunning him for what was left of his attention. In that way,
on that day, he'd rejoined the millions who went about their
business without the faintest thought of how well their bodies were behaving.

Being a non-swimmer on a regular basis, then, made me
fix on minima and lowest common denominators. Would we
know our own livers, kidneys, hearts, if we saw them? Or
those of those near and dear? Those organs' oddities
wouldn't necessarily reflect those of their owners, who could
conceivably go on "being themselves" though full of trans-
plants. Yet those organs had a dignity through sheer association: interchangeable, perhaps, on one level, on another
they were unique, even if only a bit more unique than they
were standard life-support systems. Going further, I wondered if the sight of the womb from which you came would
inspire any degree of awe, not to mention poignant nostal-
gia, whereas a glimpse of Father's penis might inspire only a
moment of lewd irreverence. There was a spectrum of devo-
tion, and taboo, in which your mother's nose counted for
more than her womb, but her womb for more than her liver,
yet these for nothing compared to her voice. All the delight
and mystery of being quick (as the ancients used to say),
and on this planet, came in two sizes: personal or general,
and you improved your sense of either by pondering the
other. Yet it was more common to extol your mother's liver,
say, because it was hers than to extol her for having a liver
at all. Far from the mere relish of organ mechanics, there
was something else, related to it of course, but almost a foul
mysticism of the liver, the lymph, the blood, the bile. This,
the substrate of the personal life—the stuff that underlies it—
struck me, in its glistening, elastic near-perfection, as the
other face of beauty, and a beauty not always decipherable
in the traditional way as distinct from what's called ugly.
The Hunchback of Notre Dame didn't have a hunchfront
too, which is to say he looked all right.

"Beauty" used to mean "blessed"; and, although orthodox
beauty was blessed (something to be thankful for, God
alone knew why), the good and the bad and even the
downright ugly were blessed too and worth being thankful

for. Brooding on Mona Lisa's pancreas, and wondering if an "uglier" organ existed and if we'd still think it "ugly" if it was actually the physical form of a superhuman from a planet that circled Barnard's Star, I kept being worried by something arbitrary and vacuous, something uninspected in the callow homage paid a pretty face, almost any sunset, almost any flower in bloom.* Creation was beautiful, period, wasn't it? Then why so bigoted a pecking order within it, pegged to an esthetics we'd never really thought about? A truly open-minded mystic would have fastened with unbiased zeal upon the magical structure of things, ditching beauty for blessedness and setting up a new criterion which, alongside orchids, lion cubs, and views of Saturn, put teeth, toenails, kneecaps, and boils and feces and gangrenous wounds. Too much? Too much for me. Odon of Cluny, a rampaging medieval chauvinist abbot, had already denounced women (not men) as bags of manure whom no thinking male would wish to embrace. Odon was a twit, of course, but unwittingly he makes us think: Do we embrace thoughtlessly, or do we somehow come to terms with the measured putrefaction we contain, and so develop a more open-minded sense of beauty? Severable beauty is a precarious thing, but that doesn't mean I'm duty-bound to kiss my sweetheart's feet because, properly reviewed, they're just as lovely as her lips. They're blessed, though. They help. They have structure. They call up certain Cézannes. Then why do I carry a snapshot of her face and not of them? Am I—are we?—altogether too selective? If we relish life *as such,* shouldn't we admire it in the round? We cannot make a tree. We cannot make a liver either. And, if we could, would we take the same esthetic pride in the liver as in the tree?

---

* "Hi, good-lookin'," runs a line in a commercial, "we'll be back to pick you up later." She does not appear, nor does she speak (I presume it's a she).

In the days when bless was *blaedsian,* it meant to smear
with blood, as if to recombine things guided apart by fear,
the word for which was *uggr,* or by indignation or even
primitive good taste. Well, I wanted them together again:
not people smeared with their own droppings, like beasts of
the field, but at least apprehensible in the same field of view
by the same criteria, and indeed smeared ritually with the
good old substrate—our planet's surface ground up into the
painter's pigments, the mucous throat that first formed
blaedsian, the unique shapes of certain bacteria first made
visible by Dr. Ehrlich's magic dye (before he dreamed up
the magic bullet too).

Maybe I'd over-responded to Keats's "'Beauty is truth,
truth beauty'—that is all /Ye know on earth, and all ye need
to know." Since I was eleven, the lines had nagged at me,
warning that the real test would be to find the beauty in the
truth rather than to figure out if what was beautiful were
true or not (who cared?). Perhaps the beauty in truth re-
sided in truth's very indeterminacy anyway. You couldn't
pin it down. But that was a sidetrack, surely, unless everything was as arbitrary as it was indeterminate. Thirty years
later, I hit on a similar sentiment in Yukio Mishima's novel,
The Temple of the Golden Pavilion, in which one character
proposes to dispense with beauty altogether, so that a club
foot might become as pleasurable an object of contem-
plation as the golden temple itself. Forced? No doubt: Museums, not galleries of art, receive the clubbed feet of this
world, in jars and not on plinths. Yet the museums comple-
ment the galleries of art, and vice versa. Truth is a constant
supplement, maybe the most blessed contaminant of all,
teaching us not to be so Manichean: to see both sides of the
miracle of life's createdness, to see things whole, giving frog
spawn and a thumbprint a chance in court against red sails
in the sunset and the *Venus de Milo.* To be Creation's eclec-
tic, neither sentimentalizing cancer by doting on tinted

slides of its cellular complexity, nor rejecting them out of
hand on the grounds of moral indignation, may be cold
comfort. At least, though, you learn Creation isn't the Big
Bad Wolf or God's Lamb but a copious self-perpetuating
process of trial and error which our essentially optional
works of art reveal even in transcending it. And the range of
those works may be much narrower than we think.

Water itself had a couple of faces for me: the pastel blue
littoral of a Bahama and the bottomless dams of my boyhood. To meet it squarely, as I kept trying to do, meant re-
sponding to it not just lyrically, which was no chore, but
subduing it through some act of will. Surely, after trying everything, I might even learn to swim by numbers, blindly
obeying what the textbook said. That was how you learned
to wield a bayonet, say, or cut a dovetail joint in carpentry.
Yet will had failed, and intelligence hadn't even been
brought into play. I couldn't force myself to swim, and I
couldn't quite come to terms with a universe that left me
out: I could no more stomach that than, in spite of all I felt
about the double face of beauty and the blessedness of everything, I could become an addict of rotten eggs. Why,
even if that gorgeous apparition in the winter skies, the
Great Nebula in Orion, smelled bad, would I like it half as
much? Thousands of times I'd peered at it through my telescope: a pale green curd lit from within by a trapezium-
shaped nursery of young blue stars. In photographs it was a
gorgeous firebird, a Nijinsky of the night. But if it stank—if
you could smell it across the light-years—would I falsify it
by ignoring its smell or ruin my esthetic fun by inhaling it
time and again in the interests of truth? I could do nothing
at all about this nebula, except on the level of adjustment,
whereas perhaps, even after thirty years of trying to swim, I
might yet prevail. There was always time and room for another try.

And, even if I ultimately failed, I'd learned something,

hadn't I? Now I knew why F. Scott Fitzgerald held a mag-
nifying glass over post-mortem photographs of hobnail liver,
that drinker's terminus: He was looking at the hard-to-
stomach beauty in the mess. I knew why the German poet-
doctor Gottfried Benn had planted a rose inside a cadaver's
opened-up chest: He was trying to shove beauty's horizon
farther and farther from the so-called norm, arguing with
himself that, to all possible combinations of things, there
must be some kind of response. Maybe theirs was the only
way of defusing horror, of coming to terms with what
makes us gag, or bellow with commonsense indignation. By
contemplating things in their most hideous aspect (what
the Greeks called *deinosis*†), you could learn to get along,
even if with only slightly lessened aversion, even if only
your mind said O.K. while your senses still recoiled. Bug-
bears never go away, and to live untraumatized you almost
have to dump the beauty of things along with the sadness of
them. *Lacrimae rerum*, says a Roman phrase for the tear-
fulness of things. Well, if you want the things, you get the
tears, and most of us get by only through developing some
sort of oblivious numbness that adds up to what those same
Romans called *aurea mediocritas*—golden mediocrity, in
which you live half-stoned or insulated like a hand in a bar-
becue glove.

No good, so far anyway, to hold my test tube of seawater
up to the light, vowing I'll get you yet. Will would have to
force itself to be casual. Will would have not to think, but
would make of me a straw, a leaf, until my atoms reached
equipoise in water. There was only one physics, wasn't
there, which was the sun's, the planet's, mine; and so, by
heeding it, I'd get my wish, even if doing so entailed a
superhuman act of will that willed me almost to the point of
passivity, and yet not all the way: I'd make myself 99 percent relaxed, but the other 1 percent would be hard at

† As in "*dino*saur."

work. There were other emotions to come, things I'd never even expected I'd feel, and other semi-rational ploys, other bits of self-deception, other circular trains of useless thought, compulsory because the more I tried to swim in water, the more I found myself out of my depth in the universe. That was the trouble. The longer you waited, the more you thought, and the more you thought, the longer you waited.

All that was left was a mindless act: jump in and risk it. Be a child, be care-less. But I cared too much, and could only come up with a wholly different answer: stop trying to swim, to tread, to float, and regard yourself as raw material, shedding all sense of self, and becoming what scientists call an artifact, by which they mean something they don't like— a flaw in a photograph, a blatantly false element in a result. I would be the thing that didn't belong, and simply report myself to myself in a state of complete unwantedness. Desperate? Yes, but I'd at least become the sole authority on what it was like to be unwanted by water, which didn't even know my name. Although sentient, I'd be the false coloration in the latest picture of Saturn, I'd be the bit of torn-off outdoor carpeting that blew up from the pool's deck into the water and, after an hour or two on the surface, began to sink. Whatever happened to me would be the result, and the preparations for the experiment said: Almost shut off will. Measure yourself as if you were a thermometer or a scale. Note every phenomenon as an instance of something, for as long as you can stand it, and accept that whatever you come up with has no bearing on the concept "swim." You are going to turn into the autobiography of a fluke, whose only consolation will be this: Both scientists and non-scientists use the same word, "artifact," to mean opposite things; it's what we like and what they don't; and you, with your shut-off will and your helpless body, are somewhere in between. You are not what *you* like, but you can make of what happens an experience you can grow to like, mainly because there is nothing else—at least under the heading "swim"—you'll ever have. On the other hand, you are not what *they* like because, in measuring and recording yourself, you are both less and more than an accurately transcribing instrument. You are going to be like Sir Isaac Newton, who almost ruined his eyes with looking at the sun's image in his looking glass and had to shut himself away for three days on end, in his "chamber made dark," to divert his imagination from the sun, and to rest his retinas as well. After three or four days, he began to regain the use of his eyes, although for months afterward he found the spectrum of the sun coming back to him, even when he lay in bed at midnight with his curtains drawn. Just to think of the sun made his retinas burn. Newton had made his eyes the raw material of his experiment, and that was good enough for me. (What he didn't seem to know, as I did from having undergone it, was that the migraine sufferer can actually bring on an attack of the ophthalmic variety merely by thinking about the visual upset which characterizes the malady.) Indeed, what better epitome of "unspoiled" raw material than Newton, the lifelong virgin, experimenting like other scientists of his day by taste testing mercury, arsenic, and other substances, even at the risk of poisoning himself, which it is said he did. Newton was his own guinea pig; his own litmus paper, reagent, indicator. Every man his own phenolphthalein, which alkalis turn red and acids blanch.

Thus fortified, with all kinds of non-status, I was ready to have at the water again. A self-reporting specimen, both self-distorting and self-fulfilling, I would be, no longer an object of praise or blame, but ripe for the squalid collection that included the man who'd composed 519 unpublished, unsung songs; the woman who'd failed her driving test 39 times; the naval officer who'd unsuccessfully stood for office 21 times; the singer who scored no points at all in the 1978

Eurovision Song Contest; and the legendary boy from my old school who'd done so badly in the Latin exam, not only getting everything wrong but also miscopying the questions into a Latin unfit for pigs, that the examiners gave him a minus percentage to damn him in this world and scalp him in the next. I even belonged to the "Gtetan Protective Association of Two Thousand Times Losers" conjured into being by SF writer William Tenn: a clique of misbehaving amoebalike creatures out on the fringe of the Milky Way. I had never realized how big (and how generous) the freemasonry of the no-can-do can be.

I belonged with Raphael Gomez, the worst matador ever, of whom Ernest Hemingway said it would be in bad taste for a bull to kill him before he yet again sprinted away and dived headfirst over the barrier. Or with Pedro Carolino, author of the worst English-Portuguese/Portuguese-English phrase book, one sample of which runs, "The dog than bark not bite; the stone as roll not heap up not foam; he eat to coaches." And with Arthur Paul Frederick who, between 1962 and 1977, patented 162 inventions, none of which was taken up commercially, including an amphibious bicycle, a back-seat-drive car, and a scheme that would shoot snowballs from the polar regions into deserts through gigantic peashooters. Also with comedienne Pat Coombs who in 1973, while making a breakfast-cereal commercial, forgot her lines twenty-eight times. And Francis Webb, the worst locomotive designer in history, who improved locomotives until they would not start at all and whose "Teutonic" class featured driving wheels that went in opposite directions. And Harvey Gartley, the boxer, who in 1977 knocked himself out after forty-seven seconds of the first round in the fifteenth Saginaw Golden Gloves Contest; actually, he fell down exhausted, but was counted out all the same.

In full flight from the ridiculous to the sublime, I began to find something unspeakably beautiful (to begin with, anyway) in the combination of water with light, water with air, akin to an older sense I'd had ever since looking through a picture window at a back-yard snowscape etched with black tracery of trees while I listened to Aaron Copland's *Appalachian Spring*. Perhaps what caused it was the same pool, muffled in sofas of snow, as much out of action then as I myself was when the pool was open; and it didn't matter that, in composing this music, the composer had been thinking mainly of something he'd like Martha Graham to dance, or that he'd written some of it in the Goldwyn studios in Hollywood, knowing nothing of Appalachia, and adding the title later on. Music was music, and *I* was the program while the music lasted. Warbles and squeaks burgeoned into mellow, dignified obeisances to spring, as if a million never-before combined shreds of unutterable tenderness had begun to melt together, making a pastel climate for the ear. And the music said: It is here, it is for you, soak it in because you are here to hear it, and the lump in your throat means you are moved simply because you are alive, and these are the sounds of sanity. That salmony-pink seepage trembling behind the trees, and tinting the snow with the faintest tones of flesh, is your own star going down. *You are living on a planet.*

It had never hit me before like that. This was how a back yard on a planet looked. Out of that dead, virtually birdless winter silence, there came welling a tremendous whoosh of joy and pride and complex tender adoration; all of a sudden I saw the dooryard as its own maker might have seen it, maybe for the first time casting a glance at that small patch among the trees, with the rectangle of the pool swaddled in its ermine snow, and noting the wholly accidental play of light on bark and roof and glass, the fallen apples frozen solid, the squirrels making fast short runs like commandos in enemy terrain, the bronze dryness of the vine. Not one of my maker's main effects by far, not when compared to the gigantic splurge of vermilion that dawdled ever-slipping in the western sky, but honorably typical, given a star, a planet, the roundness of the eyeball, a visible spectrum as wide as the one we have. I worshipped it as that which had been made, and went on being made, and would go on being made when I was nowhere at all; yet I worshipped this dark on white, touched with pink, in at least two ways: one, with the sound of Copland switched off, so that the massive frigid drone of winter could come through, in a creak, a bough sigh, a cheep from an almost-asleep bird, and I felt swallowed up in the otherness while the whole world spun to make this hue on the snow, that dot of scarlet on the horizon's needle, going, going, almost gone, even as I looked at it; whereas the other way of worshipping was with sound full blast, so the music that voiced my feelings fed them all over again, and what I worshipped then was the humanity we pour non-stop into the universe, not to humanize it, but somehow to make the mix more poignant, as if we had been brought into being only to break our hearts in the presence of a tone poem. In that expanded moment, while Copland's spring came to its crescendo in the teeth of winter's outside grip, I rejoiced in the mere fact that I had anything to be conscious of, whereas the trees, the snow, the frozen apples did not; and I said, thank God I am a witness to part of this involuntary radiance, which in hurting dazzels, which in sustaining seeds you with hopes of immortality. At least I am here to ponder it, to soak it up with appalling slowness, as if I myself were tree or snow, one of those apples not even the deer can find; I am looking at this dooryard as if there were no humans in it, or by it, or even near, as if consciousness has never been, and the whole pageant were some masterpiece of utterly unseen longevity, just brightening and darkening with the sun for as long as the sun lasts.

Chilled by such an absence from myself, I turned the

music up loud, to make the trees grow ears and get the snow to dance, budge an apple half an inch through sheer percussion. And that did it. Winter and Copland did it, ramming the lump in my throat down into my heart, so hard that I thought I'd never breathe again; I was choking on my own capacity to feel, as if dared by the snowscape in the presence of the music that loosened me up, as if dared by the music in the presence of the snowscape that told me to thaw. We are only here to feel, I told myself. No, we haven't been *put* here to feel; we feel, we happen to be here, and we are caught between admiration for the master-works of the invisible artificer and sorrow for ourselves, who, feeling as keenly as we do, credit our source with an even keener capacity to feel. A god is always more gifted than what he makes, isn't he? Or maybe not: A god is an initial force, not a final or an interim product; so, if, as we do, we do the sun's crying for it, its laughs and howls, and make its puns, are we not also doing the same for the gods who made us? Isn't there some such thing as an Omnipotent who cannot cry, in wrung elation, at the sounds of Appalachian spring mimicked on string instruments? Unable to kill the assumption, I knew I had to give it at least the time of day, and feel glad or mad or sad for whatever it was that made us and, in so doing, created almost by accident the intermittent marvels of the sensuous feast we call the local universe. The shock I felt was the difference between feeling your own almost uncontainable emotions tap you into God, or god-head, and realizing that the circuit runs only from Aaron Copland to you (and those near and dear to you), and back again. So whatever I heart-felt, so to speak, went out in a loop and returned to its source; and, even when communicated, stayed in the loop that humans make. There was something prodigiously forlorn in Copland's ecstatic cadences. They were the tremors of having. I imagined that music playing, in the same back yard, in all seasons, at a time when there were no humans left, and it was as if the music were wholly inaudible. Maybe a few birds would answer, fooled (but not for long), and then the true polarity of that music would begin: an arctic with no antarctic, endlessly repeating (as long as there was electricity) in tribute to the very thing that had no power to savor it.

No, that I could not bear. The music, I told myself, is for us, on behalf of Nature, which cannot help itself. We are the heart of things, the spawners of ecstasy, and however emotional we are is how emotional the universe is. The music of the universe, at least the solar system's, begins and ends in our own hearts. The rest is vacuum, bone, and death.

From then on, as if driven, I began to play with dense blue washes brushed from a pot of watercolor across thick white paper, not so much creating pools as inventing water, paddling my fingers in it, tilting it from corner to corner until it spilled, and marveling at the depths and shallows I could make. I explored all the textures of blue. Water was never so plastic, so holy, so impure. Pools within pools, oceans within oceans, came from my brush, even as I dreamed in a headlong voluptuous anguish of pools and oceans within a collage, and then I began to make them, with scissors, glue, and anything that came to hand. A Dixie cup was the pool, two paper clips its ladder, its winter tarpaulin a disk of see-through plastic. Before covering the pool, I painted all the water on the inside of the Dixie cup and glued a tiny model swimmer down there on the bottom, far beyond saving. Sea monsters soon followed, made from silver paper and bits of wool bound with thread. Hand-torn chunks of green kitchen paper towel had the duck-egg green of Bahamas water. A reef was a ridge of quick-dry "correction fluid," overpainted while wet with pale solutions of blue or lime. When I filled an actual sawn-off Dixie cup, or a made-over soap dish, I floated tiny electric bulbs in them for eyes or heads, wanting to thicken up and populate my watery universe that smelled of whitewash and dried seaweed. Small diving boards came out of sandpaper files worn thin by human nails and jutted out over the Prussian blue deep ends, miles beneath, and gaudy stamps from this or that Riviera began to creep into my collages, their beaches and waters dunned a little by a uniform wash of translucent brown, the easiest color to make. You just mix everything together.

Like some witch doctor with my array of effigies, I wondered if I'd managed to lift the hex from the beloved water. No pass of hand seemed apt, no uncouth chant, but what would do it—what would have to do it—was to stare at my models with undisguised fanatical yearning while I murmured *Let me in, let me in,* sinking my eyes past the plastic lid that pretended to be water and plumbing the very depths, where ultramarine met azure. Over basins of water (real this time) I flew tiny paper gliders made origami style, seeing them finally darken with wet, grow pulpy as if beginning to flower, and then become sodden, some sinking because their paper was porous, others not because their paper was different, and I half-expected, with blurred eyes, to see an escaped pilot floating close by in his dinghy. If I have to die, I told the floating paper planes, then let *me* float, then let me make friends with water. These are my tributes, these are your trophies. These are my pleas, these are your toys. Just let me in. Or down. I'll be good. I won't even ask to breathe. I'll always shower first. Let me swim, let me dive.

If I had flooded a model railroad, I'd have had better results; but I had at least pledged myself, and on I went doing just that again and again, in scores of paper baskets filled with water of all colors, little handworked scenarios of patios with umbrellas and chaises longues, done with cardboard, pins, rubber bands, and bits of death. Some I

burned, some I flooded, some I threw out for nature to
subdue with rain and beaks, but a few I kept, religiously, to
trim with paper flowers and faces cut from photographs, for
all the world as if, properly attended to, they would teach
the swim part of my brain to do its job and get me there. I
pleaded with the paper pools, I breathed heavy with yearning until the little paper umbrellas came unglued from their
stems. Tiny as a minnow, I swam at ease beneath the see-
through plastic lids. Let me swim, I told the universe of
water, and I will be yours, through and through; but I was
its already, and I had nothing to bargain with, except the
ability to read. Would I give up that?

Swim but never read again? The water was imperious.

Well, I began, flexing my shoulders . . .

Drown in your well, the world of water told me. You are
not serious.

I was, though, oh I was, and my very toes throbbed to be
in action; but all the weight of all the pools and oceans was
against me; it was in all or any of them that I could not
swim, and in none of them begin. There was something
hopelessly *wrong* with me: a gargoyle of sorts, but one
implanted in my genes, and it had scores of times given me
both the sense of vertigo and that of immersion. I had migraine, and hang-ups galore, and a head full of horrors, together with a chronic sense that, ever since I was tiny,
something had *swum through* me unbidden and unwelcome
too.

"What you have to do," said the woman who by then had
become my companion and was to be my swimming tutor as
well, "is put all that stuff out of your mind. Swimming isn't
metaphysical, it's a matter of balance, angle of repose. Physics, see? It doesn't matter what's going on in your mind
once your body's learned to float. You can think all sorts of
drowning thoughts and still stay up."

"I've tried," I said numbly. "It never works."

She planked a flat hand against the small of my back and, without the merest hint of weariness on this hundredth occasion, instructed me to lie back. "Ease back. I'll hold you. It's only four feet deep." But I didn't want to trust myself to it, the water; it would spill over me and I'd end up inhaling it. Diane had never known such fears.

"I hear you," she said. "It isn't the water you don't trust, it's me."

"No," I mumbled. "The water."

"Well," she began again, quoting Harold Macmillan, "nobody trusts a man who trusts nobody."

"Or no thing."

"Stop holding your breath. Breathe as usual."

My jaw clamped shut, and stayed so, even as I remembered that diphtheria is called that because a *diphthera,* a piece of leather in Greek, forms in the throat and chokes the victim. I told her so.

"You can breathe after all, then. Think of Archimedes if you must go Greek on me. Now, lean. Come on, back, back."

I reeled sideways and went face down, trying to crawl on hands and knees through the water to dry land. Once again she showed me how, bobbing like cork. A wedge of cork with a mane of black hair flowing beneath and behind her like a harvest of filamental seaweed. It too could float.

"I think your hand's pulling me down," I said.

"Rubbish." She showed it to me, neat and innocent.

"Let me try without." It never worked, but what the hell.

"The hand's to reassure you. Don't you need any more reassurance? That's great."

I sank again, mainly because I tried to preserve a stiff diagonal, like one of those rods that Archimedes puts into water and then observes abruptly bending. But it wasn't

Archimedes who thrashed the sea with rods, it was Xerxes.
". . . like Xerxes," I told her, gasping, blind.

"Screw Xerxes. Lean back and let the water lift you up.
You're *buoyant.*"

An hour later we had the same exchange all over again,
and she went inside to wash the chlorine out of her hair,
which I never did, eager to hold on to anything that might
make me more of a water creature.

"I'll practice," I called, but she knew that I meant I'd
paddle about, faking it, sticking a foot on the bottom just as
my trunk began to heave backward and the whole damned
operation began to become successful. What had she said
before we began? "The motel of your self-confidence should
be booked full. Then you'll float." Well, it wasn't, and it
wasn't I who took two baths a day, each an hour long, reading Colette and Saint Exupéry in a sybaritic foam of milk,
almonds, lavender, and musk. Minimum contact with water
was more than enough for me, yet I insisted on trying to
float while, from the blue-white round rib of the pool coping, she read Camus aloud on how wonderful it was to swim
in the Mediterranean and feel it take possession of his legs.
I knew the passage by heart, but it only made me morose.

"Read to me about drowning," I once said. "Maybe it'll
scare me into doing right."

"I'm not superstitious," she said, "but I won't tempt fate.
Won't egg it on."

"No such thing. There's only law and chance."

"*Float,*" she scolded me, "don't prattle."

"But prattling's a kind of oral floating."

"Then fixate it on the water, and then we can go on to
stage two."

I shook my head. Only in words could I fight water.

"Those who cannot float," she rhymed at me, "are doomed
to wade about. Roll over, Rover."

Then she suggested I use a kickboard of some sort, but I

ended up underneath it or plunging away from it as it flipped away into the air. Her hand was better, but it reminded me of a security I needed to do without; supported by the hand, I wanted to seize it and hold on to it instead of leaning back with it an inch away. Incongruous? So was having this distinguished pioneering poet as my swim tutor—rather like having Enrico Fermi as your plumber. The microscopic, roving eye that hymned our solar system in *The Planets: A Cosmic Pastoral,* a book at once strict and visionary, also had to watch me flopping and slopping about. Perhaps, I thought, whenever she sees this me, this ungainly mix of eft and seacow, she pretends she is looking at a semi-intelligent form from planetary space, to be indulged without illusions. Perhaps "Ode to the Alien," the final poem in her second book, included me too, especially when I showed no flair at all. Some of the lines, written at home, struck close to home as well. While two of them reassured me (". . . you are beautiful/until proven ugly"), the converse seemed likelier, and others posed awkward questions:

> Are you flummoxed by that millpond,
> deep within the atom, rippling out to every star?

But the last lines made a handsome gesture, appropriate for a silicon-based hominid from a planet circling good old Barnard's Star, that runaway orange dwarf in the constellation Ophiuchus, racing toward us at seventy-three miles a second:

> So, Beast, pause a moment,
> you are welcome here.

Any millpond flummoxed me, and my pausing had racked up an unseemly sum of years; but, murmuring these lines with near-obsessive glee as I splashed around out of my element, I told myself that, whenever she seemed mellowly ex-

asperated by my botched performances, she was doing her
best to gaze through me to the star stuff of my cells, fitting
me into the widest context of all. I was just another sight to
be relished during the impromptu walking tour of the universe she undertook daily, pausing here and there to marvel
at axolotls, red-capped fungi, mu-mesons, or to extract
"barium" and "radium" from "Rimbaud," imagine what
Saint Augustine would have said to Einstein, and nudge
tame rabbits in the rump.

Yet "Beast," her word for the Alien, also came from her
favorite movie, Jean Cocteau's *Beauty and the Beast*, in
which the actor Jean Marais, done up in face fur, fleecy
mane, and tusks, insists he doesn't like compliments. I was
Cocteau's Beast—that bass-voiced, clear-eyed lion whose
courtly pathos goes ill with his savage lunges at the fauna in
the park—and, far from liking or not liking compliments, I
was entitled to none. Every bit as uncouth, growling, surly
as he, I would never, as he does, turn into the presentable
prince who in the end joins Beauty in Diana's Pavilion. The
Beast in the movie shed his pelt and got the girl, the moral
of which, as the movie shows, is that without love all men
are monsters. I already had *La Belle*, the Greek or Persian
version, with long black hair, bush-baby eyes, and elegant
expressive hands. And a pass to Diana's Pavilion. But I
stayed a monster of the shallows, all grunt and spit, pout
and choke, a hairy ogre fit only to lap up pond water at the
kneel, walk on all fours, and chomp stags raw. How
different from her soft-spoken, alert cadences even while
she did the mental, imaginative equivalent of handling
liquid oxygen with her bare hands.

I brooded like this for hours. A rank amateur in the presence of something even more magical than Cocteau's recast
fairy tale, or the arrival of the Beast from Barnard's Star, I
kept trying to transform myself, to win the water's wel-
come; but an alien Beast I stayed, wrong for the planet that

was wrong for me. She had converted me to astronomy, thus consummating my lifelong passion for aeronautics, although it was galaxies rather than planets that delighted me most, and that would have to be enough. As far as water went, I was a family failure, fit only to be planted in a deep hole in solid earth and allowed to turn my face uncomprehendingly to the sun as it seemed to move.

So I fixed on Barnard's Star again, six light-years away, discovered in 1916, just west of 66 Ophiuchi, the uppermost star in the Bull of Poniatowski, heavy name for a small group of stars, otherwise known as an asterism. Who *was* Poniatowski? Who and where was he until he got his Bull? Barnard, I remembered in a waterlogged blur, was E.E., like e.e. cummings (who doted on the lower case). And *"Velox Barnardi"* (Barnard's Quickie), otherwise known as the Greyhound of the Skies, had a wiggly track as well as, according to Peter van de Kamp of Swarthmore College, two planets going around it, one of them having a mass somewhat larger than that of Jupiter, the other one somewhat smaller but okay.

This was just the big stuff that I needed, meddling in grandeur to preserve my self-esteem. The center of gravity moved uniformly through space, carrying the whole system with it. At the Sproul Observatory, Van de Kamp and two colleagues had been watching this greyhound since 1938 while it took roughly one fourth of the time it needed to creep across the sky by an amount roughly equal to the diameter of a full moon. The wiggle corresponded to the angular width of a pinhead seen ten miles away. Coming toward us all the time, this was the fastest star in the heavens and the closest lone star to the sun. Orbiting it once every twenty-six years (the lesser sibling taking twelve), Van de Kamp's big planet was one hundred times too faint to be detected by the naked eye, but just the right size and mass for a planet. It wasn't a star, it couldn't be. There were laws

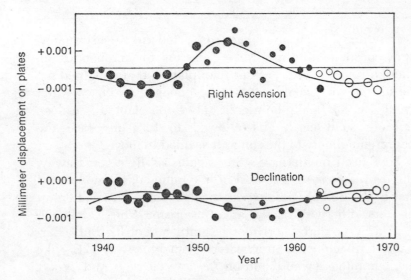

Relative proper motion of Barnard's Star. Dots proportional to the annual number of photographic measures made. Open circles represent positions since 1963.

Courtesy Peter van de Kamp.

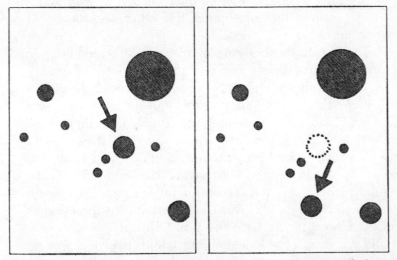

Proper motion (i.e. across the line of sight, on the night sky) of Barnard's Star, mostly northward, between 1937 and 1962, 1/15 of a degree. Selective diagram.

governing such promotions. So, the astronomer in me told
the non-swimmer, the amateur wise-guying the duffer: We
are not as alone as we thought. Maybe on that planet, you'll
find things easier. Maybe the water's cushier.

Dancing before my sealed eyes like the phenomenon
called *muscae volitantes,* literally "fluttering flies" which are
really mote- or threadlike cell fragments moving about in
the vitreous humor or the lens, the dots in a diagram of Barnard's Star—its wobble set to millimeters—floated to and fro,
as if from too much bearing down. The star wobbled and
wavered more than ever, subject to perturbations of my
own. I decided to call it the Roller Coaster Star, the Drunk
of the Heavens, a star for me as in the diagram it sank
below the zero line, rose briefly above it, then sank again,
after which mishap, in the lower part of the drawing, moving leftward, backward in time, it began above the surface
line, then as it were snorkeled for fifteen years before heaving back into view. All this, I told myself as I pretended to
learn to float, had happened between 1940 and 1970, or
thereabouts; my diagram, as well as my memory of it, was
out of date; but, taken together to form a human outline,
the two curves approximated my helpless form, with my
head over to the right in 1980, my sternum popped up high
in the region of 1953, and my rear end incongruously beneath it in the slop, with a narrower waist than I'd ever had
since boyhood. Now, as I began to feel chilly and deserted,
the black spots became the even bigger ones in two sketches
that showed the motion of Barnard's Star over a period of
twenty-five years. And moved it had, while others kept their
place, or appeared to, frozen in time like me. Yet, I reasoned, patting the blue water, if the star has moved and is
coming *toward me,* then *I* am imperceptibly moving toward
it: Only measure my proper motion aright, with sensitive
enough instruments, and you can see me budge. Not at a
standstill, a swimstill, at all.

But, in order to remember, to prolong that reverie, I had
indeed come to a halt, wondering with almost abstract gratitude who first taught me to care about such things, to
memorize the names, the numbers, the quaint saliences of
things so far away. From the first, not only the outlandish
names of certain stars had won my mind and mental ear—
Deneb, Canopus, Marfak, Fomalhaut, Zuben Elgenubi, Yed
Prior—but also the comets, those fast enormous snowballs
called Encke, Grigg-Skjellerup, Tempel-Swift, De-Vico-
Swift, Neujmin I, Schwassmann-Wachmann II, Whipple,
and West. Poniatowski's Bull, Orion's Sword, the Coalsack,
Job's Coffin, Berenice's Hair, the Lagoon Nebula, the Crab
Nebula, the Great Nebula in Andromeda, had all provided
an initial shiver of delight, almost before I knew what they
were. Had I come to astronomy through words, then?
Through names? Had there been no heavenly bodies at all,
but just the vocabulary, I might have settled for that: for
the novelty, the pageantry, not unlike reading the telephone
directory in a foreign town.

Of course there was more to it, as I think I first realized
when pondering the near-hypnotic appeal of such proper
names as Kapteyn's Star, Van Maanen's Star, Van Bies-
broeck's Star, and Barnard's Star of course, but most of all
stars called Lalande 21185, Lacaille 8760, Krüger 60, One-
Zwicky-One, Wolf 359, and Groombridge 1830. Unlikely
names, mingling both the exotic and the prosaic, they somehow gave me a whiff of the familiar at the heart of the
remote. Imagine suns, I incredulously told myself, every single bit of which belongs to Groombridge, Wolf, or Zwicky.
Numbers and Greek letters didn't work half as well; I was
savoring human culture at random in the hinterland of an
unthinkable vastness, and actually to locate one of these stars
(or whatever else), trap it in the telescope and murmur its
preposterous name was to find a backdoor poetry. The stars,
I persuaded myself, had the personality evoked by their

names, although many of the Arabic names came from the star's place in the figure devised for its constellation: in Scorpius, for example, Dschubba meant "the front of the forehead," creamy white Al-Niyat "the outworks of the heart," and Shaula "the sting." Rotanev, however, was the reversed Latinized surname of Niccolo Cacciatore, a modest astronomer (though one of my reference books haplessly noted "meaning unknown"), while Svalocin (or Sualocin), a dusky greenish dwarf also in the constellation Delphinus, was "Nicolaus" given the same treatment. Rarely had anything so verbal come linked with things so inhumanly and irrefutably aloof. I had found a treasure trove of Adamic naming, along the lines of the Hebrew letter for Jehovah, but much more entertaining, unpredictable, a word-hoard locked away in the treasure box of the sky.

Invited a few years ago to suggest Oriental and African authors as names for the craters on Mercury, some friends and I came up with scores of them and sent them in to the appropriate international committee. Most of our suggestions flopped, but with Lady Murasaki we prevailed, and she now resides between Homer and Bach, an immigrant. Out there, scorched by the local star, the eleventh-century Japanese author of *The Tale of Genji* humanizes a hollow, a dent, between Odysseus and those forlorn tenors in Bach's cantatas who embody the soul addressing itself to God. Later on, after my first crush abated, I began to deal maturely with astronomical references, learning to prize even certain figures, such as the Messier numbers (though I still prefer "Sombrero Galaxy" to "M 104"), the X-ray source Cygnus X-1 (candidate for a black hole), and 3C-273, perhaps the brightest and nearest quasar, sprewing a tongue of matter maybe 150,000 light-years long, which sounds big until you realize it wouldn't even reach from the sun to the Magellanic Clouds. If you keep up with astronomy, you join Lewis Carroll's White Queen in believing at least six impossible things before breakfast daily. The knowledge, the guesswork, is enchanting, but the nomenclature is bizarre heraldry in its own right, ever-increasing; and in my perverse way I relish getting to know the names—names that stick—for things the experts can't always quite fathom. I had even helped myself to one of their mnemonics—"Oh, be a fine girl, kiss me now"—to murmur in the pool, more or less to the tune of "Oh, give me a home where the buffalo roam," rarely remembering the star colors that the initial letters (O, B, A, F, G, K, M, N) stood for—electric-blue, blue, blue-white, yellow-white, yellow, orange, red, and "cool" red, but getting something soothing from the ditty all the same.

My reverie was running out of steam. The water challenge had not gone away. I could murmur the names of things bright and beautiful, but I still had to learn that knack of not going under all the time. Water-tortured, I let my mind linger on things of fire, and their puzzling neighbors. Pretending in some primal dream that I was a creature from the waters making its first foray on land, I heaved and bobbed in my bogus natural element, letting my evasions run themselves out, passing up the round Zion of the water bead for the goings-on near Barnard's Star. I doted on triumphs at a distance because they relieved me of an obligation to succeed, so to speak, as a member of the local group. Peter van de Kamp's dark planet was the first to be discovered since Clyde Tombaugh found Pluto in 1930. It was also the first known planetary companion of another sun. What a radiant extension of ourselves, or rather what a lovely enigma to tease otherworldly yearnings with. I remembered, though, being told that even the meticulous, minute measurements made of Quickie's Wiggle were open to a measure of doubt. One set of tests showed no evidence for planetary motion at all. I did not want to believe it, and I filled my head with how those two planets were rather closer to their star than Jupiter and Saturn are to ours. Why, according to two other astronomers called Suffolk and Black, there was even a third planet, almost Jovian in size and virtually whizzing around the star in only six years. All I wanted was to *know*. I tried fixing on something else, but Barnard's haunting star came back, and I knew I would journey there as slowly as learning to use water; but, first, find someone compatible to go there with, for whom not even the light-years of the beginner swimmer are too long. *Hello*, I said with my mouth chock-full of universe. "I've swum enough today. I'll try tomorrow." I had been goofing off, and I felt nine years old. Whether my mind or my mouth was open or closed, my tutor had not heard my explanation, my excuse, my literal alibi—I had been elsewhere, in Ophiuchus.

There she was at the screen door, head swathed in a turban of towel, miming the lean-back I should do, urging me to let go, to let water do the rest. How long had she been there?

"You haven't got the feel of the water yet."

"How long does that take? A lifetime and a half?"

Her answer was a slowly shaking head, whether in repetitious rebuke or awe at the time required I didn't know. Next thing she was gesturing with a small, unpainted model plane, behind the picture window, making the dun-gray *Widgeon* seem to land in stalling attitude, and I thought I might just manage to float if lowered gently into water like a seaplane landing on a two-step flared or fluted hull. My head was full of analogies for what I couldn't do, and there stood a woman with four degrees unable to help, unable to make the water feel to me as it would only after I'd committed myself to it. For all my body knew right then, water would no more hold me up than air would, and that was an outright slander too. To get me to this point of water failure, she'd had me slimmed and conned me into running a mile a day. No wonder she couldn't bear to watch me do any more of my slow, heavy, frantic slides: DuBuffet's *Pink Man* going down for the count.

Off she went to ride at the local stables while I bounced on tiptoe, hoping perhaps to bungle even that and so have a mishap get me launched.

2. A TROUGH IN TIME

Solids heavier than a fluid will, if placed in the fluid, sink to the bottom. . . .

ARCHIMEDES,
On Floating Bodies

. . . we may not disbelieve the stories told about him, how, under the lasting charm of some familiar and domestic Siren, he forgot even his food and neglected the care of his person; and how, when he was dragged by main force, as he often was, to the place for bathing and anointing his body, he would trace geometrical figures in the ashes, and draw lines with his finger in the oil with which his body was anointed, being possessed by a great delight, and in very truth a captive of the Muses. And although he made many excellent discoveries, he is said to have asked his kinsmen and friends to place over the grave where he should be buried a cylinder enclosing a sphere, with an inscription giving the proportion by which the containing solid exceeds the contained.

PLUTARCH ON ARCHIMEDES
(*Lives:* Marcellus, XVII 4–7)

Long ago, as if in a newspaper headline that got longer the more I thought about it, the poet Shelley had given me a clue. In Italy with his friends Byron, Williams, and Trelawny he was discussing a boat they wanted built; Trelawny had produced a model of an American schooner. The full-size boat would have to be thirty feet long, said Shelley, and undecked. *No: longer*, said Byron, and *decked* as well. So two boats had to be built, Shelley's based not on the American one after all but on another model Williams had brought with him from England.

Sprawled on the banks of the Arno, Shelley and his mariner cronies drew lines in the sand to represent the boat's contours and compartments; and then, with a chart of the Mediterranean spread out in front of them in their make-believe cabin, they planned the first few cruises, talking of Bligh, Diaz, and Drake while Byron stood skeptically by, wondering aloud how much salvage he would get when his own boat towed Shelley's into port. Then Shelley said plaintively, *"Why can't I swim?"* and Trelawny, who was as agile in water as a dolphin, agreed to teach him. Shelley stripped at speed and jumped into the Arno, landed on the bottom, and made no movement upward, but lay sprawled there like a conger eel. When Trelawny hauled him out, Shelley got his breath and told him, "I always find the bottom of the well, and they say Truth lies there. In another minute I should have found it, and you would have found an empty shell. It is an easy way to get rid of the body."

Yet this poet confided to Trelawny he knew nothing about the survival of the soul: "We know nothing," he said, "we have no evidence; we cannot express our inmost thoughts. They are incomprehensible even to ourselves." I brooded often on Shelley, that wraith tempted by an abstraction's ghost, who doted on drowning and in October 1819 wrote "entreating everybody to drown themselves; pretending not to be drowned myself when I *am* drowned; and, lastly, *being* drowned." It was Shelley who, at Bracknell and on Hampstead Heath, and wherever else he could find pools or ponds with firm, clean banks, sailed little flotillas of paper boats, sometimes even folded-up from letters that happened to be in his pockets, and occasionally set fire to them. He would like to be shipwrecked in one of them, he said; he had gone up-Thames in his day to find the river's source, and he had gone up and down the Arno in a flat-bottomed boat of lath and pitched canvas, such as duck hunters used in the marshes, and he had even proposed a moonlight trail trip along the canal to Pisa, which ended in disaster when Williams, suddenly standing up under the huge sail filled with wind, grasped the mast to steady himself. Into the wide and deep canal they all went, with Williams (who swam a little) managing to reach shore, while Henry Reveley grabbed Shelley, told him to be quiet and calm while being saved. "All right," Shelley said. "Never more comfortable in my life, do what you will with me." When they reached the shore, Shelley fainted, but was soon exulting in the memory: "Our ducking last night," he wrote to Reveley, "has added fire instead of quenching the nautical ardour which produced it. . . ."

Shelley was my Mister Facing-Both-Ways: the undying drowner, the drowning survivor, the water-illiterate posing as master mariner and flirting with water, teasing it, goading it, to come and get him:

> A restless impulse urged him to embark
> And meet lone Death on the drear ocean's waste;
> For well he knew that mighty Shadow loves
> The slimy caverns of the populous deep.

Those slimy caverns of the populous deep: how well I knew
them in imagination, like waves

. . . which lately paved his watery way
Hiss round a drowner's head in their tempestuous play.

I too had heard the sea "Breathe o'er my dying brain its last
monotony," but I had never pushed my luck as far as
Shelley had, on the Irish Sea, crossing the Channel with
Mary in an open boat, at Meillerie with Byron, and, out in
the bay off Lerici in his skiff with Mrs. Williams and her
children, exclaiming "Now let us together solve the great
mystery!" and scaring her to death. It was Shelley lying
doggo on the Arno's bed, rather than the corpse cast up on
the beach near Via Reggio with his volume of Sophocles in
one pocket and his doubled-back Keats in the other, who
gave me the clue. Was that what to do? Kill dread by not
resisting? How deep was that Arno anyway? Not very deep,
Mary Shelley had said. How long was he down? Had he really not held his breath but acted as if gilled? Had he just
been testing Trelawny? Was it an impulse or was it
planned? How had it felt? Why had he never learned to
swim, but remained an aquanaut of winsome, lethal water?
I had already gone this route myself, not weighting little
paper fireboats with halfpennies on the Serpentine or the
Primrose Hill Pond, to be sure, nor telling a Henry Reveley
about the boat a-building: "The rullock, or place for the oar,
ought not to be placed where the oar-pins are now, but
ought to be nearer to the mast; as near as possible, indeed,
so that the rower has room to sit. In addition let a false keel
be made in this shape, so as to be four inches deep at the
stern, and to decrease towards the prow. It may be as thin
as you please." This was only three days after the ducking
from which Reveley had saved him; but, so far, no Reveley
had had to fish *me* out, as distinct from my little yachts, my
own paper boats, paper gliders, an occasional fallen kite;

and unlike Shelley I had not seen a naked child rise from
the sea and clap its hands in glee, except for children who
trod water.

But water lore, yes. Liquid lore too. And water obsession.
All feeding a weird selfless hypnosis in which I seemed to
tread in Shelley's watery footsteps, but through a nightmare
very much my own, in which the bigger I grew the smaller
I felt. It was the beginning of the childhood I've had every
year of my adult life, and every year more vivid.

With the frail glass beaker in one hand, full of water, and
the labeled test tube in the other, I might have been the
first to do it. Taking a pinch, I dropped the crystals into the
water. Clots of cobalt swelled and broke, spewing baby
streamers up and down, which then fanned out. I was seven
for most of that year, but the chemistry set was always new,
rustling and rattling all the way from last Christmas: a port-
manteau of stinks, a double tray of lotions, with a cardboard
niche for everything to fit into. I carried the box flat, but
sometimes stood it on its side, with the lid off, like a
bookshelf, waiting for the cans of powders, the bottles of
salts, the sentry-stiff test tubes, the pipette and the mixing
rod, to tumble down; but they never did.

The world was safe, and I knew I wouldn't soar away
from the planet when I jumped upward; and, most important of all, the heavenly blue fluid I kept in its own jam jar,
sealed tight as last year's loganberries with a rubber-ring
lid, wouldn't flow down from the windowsill at night,
along the cold linoleum floor, and up between the sheets,
brushing my toes with a rounded wave front that wanted
me to drown on tiptoe, eyes just above the hem of the comforter, but my nose and mouth inhaling the blue until it ran
out of my ears, its duty done, its color flecked with froth. I
was glad.

I ogled the blue solution, and made it by the gallon in

buckets and pails and jars and cans, telling myself it had no
power to roam, to boil, to talk, or even to recite its verbal
history. I had begun, like gluttons and boozers and dyna-
miters and tree surgeons, to master the world, and to know
that it was truly more wonderful than any dread of it could
be. I became the almost proud proprietor of my dread. I
knew that all the stuff around me sucked me down, most of
the time anyway, and I tried to surrender to that feeling,
joking while drowning, winking while choking, stifling both
the joke and the wink with a practiced twitch of the mind,
like a mayfly pulsing on an iceberg. And I discovered, ever-
lastingly at home with dictionary and chemistry set, pretending to be too sick to go to school, I didn't have to *try*.
When you've given yourself back to the universe, you don't
need a passing grade. Or so I thought, until I caved in, did
what parents and teachers told me to do, and began to work
for a dying instead.

Yet the delicious aversion to liquids lingered on, and actually to swim in one—to frolic, to cavort, water bug or
water puppy—remained a dream unopened, like flying,
South America, or grown-up sex. I paddled, of course, in
tidal pools or the knee-deep shallows, sometimes heaving
full-length sideways or blundering into a trench that took
me down to nipple depth. I even rowed out to sea, maybe
forty yards, in a rented boat after first rehearsing on the
three-feet depths of the lake in a local park, happy as if I
were over seventy thousand fathoms. Why my parents let
me go, I never knew, but they believed devoutly in wood,
which didn't conduct electricity; and, since neither of them
could swim or had even tried to learn, death by drowning
was a remote affair restricted to typhoons in the China Seas
or to the careless, such as Gerald White, who worked in my
grandfather's butcher's shop and, one day, trying to save a
sheep stranded in a flooded pasture, stepped into the river
and was washed away. What was left of him reappeared a

month later, a mile away. So a boy in a rowboat, on a sea
deep as the Himalayas were high, seemed to them in less
jeopardy than on the invisible brink of a three-fathom river.
The scale was wrong for a disaster. Ships went down where
individuals did not. The boat was much heavier than I was.
It had never drowned; boats didn't drown; and, anyway, I'd
paid pocket money for an entire hour, a chunk of time that
seemed to them, and to me, invulnerable. You died or
drowned during an hour you hadn't paid for, or during an
ocean voyage for which you'd paid too much. Was that the
logic of their allowing me, frail and curly haired, alone on
the main that had munched up thousands of fishermen? No:
As long as they kept an eye on me, these two non-
swimmers, all would be well, and of course it turned out
well too, since I returned, let the boatman beach the boat,
and skipped away, as shiveringly glad as when the barber's
hands had let me go again, sending me home shorn and
plastered with sweet oils that made my hair as stiff as year-
old cow flop.

I avoided immersion at all costs, much as others avoid
talk; but I kept on peering into the still water behind the
rusty railings down Gashouse Lane, where the gasholder
rose and sank in a fat round pit full of oily water that
reeked of baby cribs. How deep was it? Was the water poi-
sonous? Did they ever change it when it had lost its powers
of flotation? Marveling at the sheen on the water which the
slow motion of the holder never blurred, I knew the gap between the tank and the wall was too narrow for a body; but
for a leg, an arm, it was just right, and my teeth began to
chatter whenever I got that close, on sunny days seeing my
face all shrunken on the surface, and on sunless ones seeing
no sign of myself at all, as if I had already slithered down
the gap, fitting my corpse to the curvature of the sides.

Even there, of course, a model yacht would have floated
easily, as if the water had no underneath. Or paper boats,

and luckless folded-paper planes, and ducks, twigs, balls, and what I didn't know were condoms, though I'd often seen them in the sea or local streams, like resected lengths of bowel adrift from the main body, their nose-blown nipple heads half full. But water was too full of dizzy givingness for me. A dunked foot went down and down; the space it left behind it then filled up again, indifferent to your last night's dream. It belonged, this water, to a secret society whose other member was air, whereas fire—purring and snapping, a bloodshot terminal moraine unto itself—was as familiar as Christmas morning. It said hello, come in and *koosh*, which is Manx for warm your loins.

Something inhuman scared me half to death, and what it was doesn't recur in the right order; back it pours with the squeal of a drowning bagpipe whose bag is a lung. The boy's foot in the marsh, where pale blue eggs nestled in a floating cup of straw, was the foot thrust past the pale blue beach spiders of Como into the top of the unthinkable depths. Flirting with vertigo, suction, or the obliging hydraulics of the Dead Sea, I relived my bout with pneumonia, brought on by playing soccer in the rain. Before coming round enough to choke into an enamel bucket for an entire month, I flickered on beneath a silver suffocating cloud which puffed up and engulfed me, cramming my head's holes with lukewarm flocks until, even through the coma, it had tweaked back to life the chronic dread of drowning. Even while half-giving up the ghost, I yearned to die choked by that cloud, and not pumped full of water.

To distract The Self (which hardly existed) from Self's inanity, the person who's writing this sentence used to address himself as *you* and, when that proved extreme (too positive a view of the fiasco), as *one*, which really wiped somebody, hardly anybody, out. The same preoccupation, neurosis, blight (whatever it was) returned when "I" looked at Descartes's famous formulation, *cogito, ergo sum*, which

used to mean *I think, therefore I exist,* but which more in-
structively translated into *There is consciousness, therefore
someone might be.* In English, to begin with "I" presup-
posed the conclusion of the statement, whereas in Latin the
personal element, the pronoun suffix, didn't show up until
the third syllable. So, for the whole of *cogit,* there was some
doubt as to who was *cogit*ing, if indeed anyone at all; the
process was, so to speak, out on its own like a lost dog without a collar; and when the *o* came up, it limited things a lot,
and not without some sense of restrictive disappointment.
Safer to say *If there's thinking, there is a thinker,* and leave
it at that, without going into all the shadow-boxing folderol
of who is who. Identity, long before I even aspired to one,
seemed to me an act of rash conjecture, because to be alive
was to be mostly in the flux, with only rare moments in
which a bit of head appeared above the swill. The universe,
I decided, dealt with us not as if we were people, but as if
we were never separate from it, and identity was one of
those soothing human myths invented to torment ourselves
with. Instead of going flat out to *be somebody* (in the
blackmail phrase that causes ulcers, cardiac arrest, and long
sojourns in the padded cell), it was more healthful, wasn't
it, to take undue pleasure in the few moments of random
autonomy? Rainbows came and went.

Anyone that immersed, or feeling that immersed, and not
resenting it, shouldn't have wanted to float or swim; so,
clearly, I wanted out, I wanted some degree of control, and
my precious mystical saturation was in part a pose. I felt I
belonged to the great big chemistry set a sight too much,
and I knew that, even if I became the best swimmer since
Odysseus, I'd never be wholly free. After all, the matrix included swimming as well; swimming was part of physics, so
what looked like an escape, an act of treason, was merely
another way of proving my entrapment. The logical thing,

therefore, was to ferret out more of the laws I had to live by, and grin and bear them.

There was another aspect to swimming too. Over and above the private sense I had of the cosmos, there was the social figure I cut, and that mattered just as much; I didn't just live in the universe, I lived in a street and went to a school, where, although you didn't exactly need an identity, you had to pass muster. Not to swim, as distinct from being able to hit, throw, or catch a ball, say, made you a booby, from top to toe; indeed, lower than a dog, who at least knew how to paddle, or a waterman, who knew how to skate across the surface tension; or even a water hen, which floats; a water soldier, which keeps its flowers above the surface; and watersheds, water tigers, waterwheels, water witches; kindred beings, all, could I but join them in the happy miscellany of adjustment. The urge was social, and so the answer to water wings, life belts, all forms of fakery, was: Not in a month of Sundays.

For years I'd polished my equivalent of a *Eureka!* speech. My head had slummed through all the dry docks of the infinite. The universe was as familiar to me as eggs on toast. Where others, goaded by poets or theologians or The-End-of-the-World-Is-at-Hand loudmouths who haunted the streets and knocked on the door, kept trying to see everyday life, under the aspect of eternity, I kept trying to see eternity under the aspect of everyday life, with a space in my diary, year after year, going unused, requiring only a brief bout in the water that entitled me to scrawl, copperplate, under the date and the name of the day: "Swam for first time." It wasn't, like an audience with God, something to brace yourself for, to dress up for, but right here on tap within a multiplicity of magically ordinary atoms which, the same as those that kept the stars on fire, guaranteed certain goings-on upon the planet might continue going on: no hitch.

So why such poor results? I wasn't short an arm, a leg; I
was wiry and athletic; I could sprint enough to win a race.
Did the hivey skin recoil? No, water contact soothed; even
the semi-abrasive lave of the sea. Then what? Drowning?
Not really. I was close to that already, and to drown would
have been the merest shimmy sideways. So perhaps it was
excess that put me off, as if being possessed by water (as by
air and earth) were an unnecessary metaphor for what was
already going on; I wanted to swim, but according to
different laws from everybody else. To drown, I reasoned,
was to go the whole hog in an idiom already well learned,
whereas to swim in the orthodox way was to be unimagina-
tive. Death by drowning was the last act, whereas to swim
was the first act of many, all of them alike. And, if death
was the merest touch extreme for anyone with such an oceanic sense as mine, that didn't matter because no one talked
about the quality of your deadness, whereas everyone cared
about the quality of your life. Drowning abolished the problem, then, but swimming made it new every morning, and I
wanted to swim unmystically and non-hydraulically. Over it
and over it I went, telling myself that such notions as
"swept away," "down for the third time," and "lost without
trace," were mere decorative finials to the porousness of
things, while my toys—the model train set, the balsa planes
that flew on wings of dope-tautened tissue paper larded
with banana oil, the lead hussars and plastic Comanches—
seemed bubbles only, ever ready to disperse and recombine
their atoms into something else—creatures whose names I'd
have to invent.

Other youths jumped in and swam, and that was that; I
had thought much too much about the thing I couldn't do,
or bring myself to do, and the problem was fast becoming
not the inability to swim but the inability to stop thinking
why? Maybe someone should have shoved me in. A matador
of the blue water, I persisted in thinking I could think my-

self to the right point and go. Physics hadn't changed, so
the problem was in the mind, and that was where I went on
grappling with it, dismissing death as a marginal flop, wanting the laws of life to be different, wanting even to walk on
water or to grow gills. Because I couldn't swim in the orthodox way, I wanted nature to come up with an unprece-
dented way in which to do it: a way just mine, which would
baffle everyone else at least as much as swimming baffled
me. Life went on. I marveled at how much I could relish
being alive without going anywhere or doing anything. Eye
watered. Nose blocked up. Lip twitched. Wrist ached. Knee
cracked. Belly gurgled. It was like being a tree. I was my
own sky, my own desert, my own ocean, even. Had I
dreamed the impossible dream of using an unused part of
my brain in order to swim as no one had swum before? Was
I to be the first to break the laws of physics, becoming a sin-
gularity without rhyme or reason? What I wanted was inhuman swimming, an oceanic experience at least as inhuman
as death: none of that exact and deliberate discipline going
all the way from Tarzan of the Apes to Captain Webb.

I had not marched up to the stage at school assembly,
along with all the other kids, to receive my swimming
certificate for Beginner Width; but I was into the marvelous, the unknown, and they were not. My abstinence tinged
with cowardice flirted with the unspeakable as well; I
wanted to be able to say I'd swum, but I suspected that the
experience, when it came, would not be ravishing enough.
Between twenty and thirty, I was convinced that such was
the explanation: not fear, not awkwardness, but the pawn-
broked mysticism which, using erotic terms to express the
unattainable unknown, suddenly finds the eroticism will be
the better of the two. Or I was like some medieval lover,
howling in a tower for consummation, who all of a sudden
shuts his mouth, thinking this pain, this longing, might well
be a keener thrill than having what I want. Or whom.

Through some flukes, the one experience I'd saved for later got right out of hand on the level of impassioned guesswork. My imagination had painted me into a corner in which I knew, I just knew, that swimming, when it came, would be an anticlimax, and I began to steer away from the very thought of it, unloading all those fond prophetic similes heated by deprivation and shame to fever pitch. I went back to my old earth-ecstasy, the ecstasy of air, telling the flux I wasn't going to hassle it anymore; I'd rest content with what I had, drowning in dry phenomena, no longer haunted by the splash of a distant sea, the pale blue water that lolled and waited in all those doctored pools.

By poetically just reversal, the matador quit the arena, self-booed and bombarded by spectators' cushions, despairing of a bull to fit his bill. The buoyant I had gone, afloat in another continuum, on another time line, and all that remained, at least in the world of humdrum explanations, was the handy lie: I'm too ungainly, I just can't seem to find the knack. I am the only would-be floating body that has no Archimedean point.

Some people, I told myself, had no timing, some no depth perception, some no manual finesse. Some couldn't dance, and some not sing. I wasn't a freak after all, and so I began to prefer the longing to the feat. For the next ten years, I smoked and read by water, but I hardly dipped a toe. When you have shed such an intellectual, sensuous overload as I had built up over thirty years, you settle for the quiet pastimes, telling yourself that in your day you've done it all, and none of it came up to snuff. Only a stride away, babes just recently in arms hurled themselves into water much deeper than they were tall and screamed as they smashed its level glaze and disappeared.

Such feelings came to life again, a century and a half after Shelley's death, when I did a grown-up Arno of my

own in yet another Florida pool, still wholly unable to swim
or even float. Breath held, I stood, walked, made the water
come over my head by kneeling groggily, and then on half-
floaty all-fours trudged along the bottom, surrounded by the
clank-snort sounds of anesthesia, and feeling like a humbled
frog, seeing only the good old copper sulfate solution, which
stung the eyes. The source of dread, I realized, was not the
bottom but the depth above it; not being down there but
going down there; not state but process. Then, with an awkward reel, I stood, shoved off at an angle, and found myself
in perfect drowning position with no breath left and no one
to help. I was forty-five years old, sole witness of an impassioned extreme in five feet of water, not having advanced as
far as I'd supposed down the rough-painted glacis that led
to the really deep water of the diving basin. I stood up and
slow-motioned away from the scene of yet another fiasco,
pretending to swim back with agitated, crooked-arm
splashes which didn't fool the tots in that vicinity, who saw
only a panicking thrasher, his rigorous grin that of the
grown-up fake. Back by the slop channel, I carefully de-
ployed my limbs, my profile, as if I weren't Shelley after all,
but Byron himself, fresh from swimming the Hellespont and
needing a breather, a bake in air's oven, before crossing it
again.

By then I had certain passages of the sea-loving Camus
by heart; Diane had seen to that, trying to make me see
how the swimmer was no longer himself, or anyone. Anath-
ema to me, of course, Camus's rapture hadn't come out of a
junior chemistry set, but from boyhood swims, and *sea* was
one of his favorite words. I doted on self-possession,
whereas he enjoyed being sapped or stolen, rapt or giddied.
Being horizontal in water was as unnatural to me as having
mercury in my veins, whereas he reveled in it, finding it not
absurd at all, but the wine that went with the sea's
indifference. If I wanted to swim before I turned fifty, I

would have to let go, and not just in my mind; I would have to let the water have its way with me, not like a crustacean, scuttling along the bottom, but up there in water's ether, where you flew, did glides, or just lolled like someone weightless on the grass. My next attempt was home again, up north.

There, scotch-taped to the ladder at the shallow end, words and facts to hearten me awaited, typed on an out-size index card, but not enveloped in plastic like those cards the scuba divers take down. So I read it at the ladder, then read it again, that billet-doux anthology of heartening lore from all across the ages, aimed to make me brave:

Remember the great swimming feats in *Beowulf*. But note that, before the sixteenth century, nobody wrote down what sorts of strokes they used (nobody knows how they swam). So you are earlier than that century in this. One early means was called the "human stroke" —alternate arm thrusts forward and down, and down-thrashes of the legs. Try it, *Etwas* [one of my nicknames, deliberately vague, meaning "something" or "anything"]. Or the dog paddle, misnamed. Good for short distances only, which is no doubt why the Slavic peoples used it—no big bodies of water to deal with, just rivers. Primitive peoples, however, all evolved the same stroke: hand over hand, like using hands for paddles after paddles have been lost. When hand-over-hand was introduced to England in 1873, by one Trugden, who got it from the North American Indians, the Brits named it the "Indian stroke." Main thing, though, is the bas-reliefs in the Nimroud Gallery of the Brit Museum: Assyrian war scenes with soldiers swimming streams either with mussuks (inflated skins) or mussuk-*less*, like you. Remember the Coin of Abydos, on which Leander very elegantly swims the Hellespont, hand over hand, while Hero stands in her tower with a lighted lamp to show the way. A.D. 193. More lore later. Think of me as Hero, *avec lampe.* Stay in the shallow end. Have to go. *Studenten* await me with their poems. Warm up the Italian bean casserole, and it's O.K. to scatter the onion rings on first so long as you don't overcook. Love, Hero.

P.S. Watch this space. You are not the first although you sometimes look as if you are. Homo sapiens awkwardissimus. Be good.

P.S. If more data needed, consult the *Red Cross* book, which is better than you know. And eat *moderately.*

I read it slowly, almost more inclined to go and sample the Red Cross book than to flop around where I was least competent; but then, after a salute crisp and even in the vague direction of Beowulf, the Indians, Nimrod, Leander, and above all Hero, I slithered in, thinking you never realize how hot your body is until you dunk it bit by bit.

Lifting one leg in four feet of water, with mind as blank as I could make it, I felt some current lift it higher than I'd wanted, like the arm freed from six months in a plaster cast: a wand of balsawood. So, the laws had not worn out. But, with arm outspread to make a monoplane of me, I dared not lift the other leg. I hopped in place, in isinglass or gruel, and with slow, vacating heaves the acrid water let me rise and fall; first with my lifted leg in front, and then behind, ready to kick a ball. Breath held or not, I felt lofted, but still I couldn't budge the other leg. When at last I converted the top of my hop into the lift-off of my other leg, I stalled and veered, then went sideways under, gulping with panic and ferociously telling myself that this was an experiment, and I its raw material. *See what happens. Don't be anyone*

at all. I tried again, letting the high leg droop this time as
the other lazed toward it, and so managed an ungainly sitting position, and the time after that only a backward yaw
that took me headfirst down, still insisting that I must
watch myself as if I were a total other. In midriff depth, I
finally discovered, my feet hungered for the bottom and
wanted to walk, whereas, of course, the plane that counted
was the water's top, and it was by that that you lined up
your body—along, athwart, like something embossed, or the
pattern in the blade of a Damascus knife, wavily welded in,
damasquiné, unable to escape.

My encore was at nipple depth, in which I'd actually
done a kneel, years earlier when I was brave, but none of
that old audacity paid off now; I did a slow-motion skid,
losing my bearings altogether, stranded between the need
to stand up and the impossible feat of lying flat on top. This
time I was right under, backside on the bottom with my
legs at forty-five degrees, enraged at forgetting to hold my
breath. I'd exclaimed something into the water, and that
was that. Again I stood, blinking sticky prisms away and
hacking from the chlorine in my throat. My body was like
some old-fashioned Chinese cangue around my neck, drag-
ging me down, wasting whatever sense of balance I had,
and not even helping me to float. Hapless prisoners,
dumped into shark-infested pools by sadistic warlords, with
their wooden cangues still bolted under their chins, had
floated head up while bitten from beneath. I deserved no
better fate myself, I thought; I'd lost my experimenter's
poise already.

After a ten-minute, seething retreat to the shallow end, I
tiptoed back to nipple depth, as willing to drown as to go
on, and suddenly retracted both legs at the knee, an air-
plane that had just taken off. Everything happened slowly
then as I rolled backward like an out-size ball, this time with
breath held rigid while I sank. Ignorant as I was, I had no

idea I could have groomed any one of these flounderings
into the first stroke of a swim, rolling into correct alignment
in a trice, reaching out for the invisible trophy which water
only too readily gave, letting my legs float upward like
flotsam from a foundered submarine. Instead, I stood, shook
off the whole pretense of trying to learn water, and smacked
the rocking surface in rebuke, glad that no one was there to
see. Even as I did, I knew I'd learned something that earlier
bungles hadn't brought. The water was somehow solid, it
had smackable bulk, a rump that waltzed away and actually
resisted motion through it. So why would it not hold me up?
What was the catch? Cupping water in my hands, I made it
squelch away, but not before I'd felt its bulge, its bulk,
squeezing it like the syrup in a sachet of shampoo and
recalling how, when a student at Columbia, I'd bought margarine at Joy's supermarket on Broadway and kneaded the
pack until the spot of scarlet dye had yellowed the ec-
toplasm within. A spot of intensest cobalt blue (the blue
with a "kobolt" or dwarf in it) would tint the entire pool;
my copper sulfate trance came back, the bright blue crystal
blued the water in the flask, and all of a sudden, out of that
conjured blue, things came together.

Water wasn't a mere transparency from here, where I
lived, to there, where I drowned; or something opaque, or a
sloppy form of nothingness. It was the slack balloon of itself, a thinner margarine in which, *amidst* which, if you
took the trouble you could whoosh forward like a wing, and
the water like air would split in front of you and shove you
up or down depending on how you angled your body. I
trapped another sample in the eggcup of my palms and,
firmly rooted near the plump chromium pipes of the shallow
ladder, squashed it back and forth, making it suck and
squeak, maneuvering it gently and thinking we have no
word for this sensation, just as the Romans had lacked one
for the ripple in the biceps when they flexed an arm, and so

had invented "muscle," which meant a mouse—a *mus*—had seemed to run along beneath the skin. I turned my head against the kingdom of the word, and gave myself over to how excited and enthralled I felt.

Two feet deeper, while red cardinals scooted about among the pink Japanese roses and the July sun baked my hair, I suddenly felt good. Water was neutral after all. You could cup it, slice it, bully it, make it support you for life. I began, almost out of my depth and gigglingly foolish, to reinvent my water history, my lips level with that swaggering line. The chlorine aroma was thick as smoke. The cardinals and jays and blackbirds took no notice, nor the squirrels on the deck. A chipmunk made its absentminded chirp, erect on the lip of a spittoon filled with red geraniums. A pheasant barked in the woods. A couple of mallards cruised over, making a leathery flap. A wren whizzed out of a green birdhouse wired to a low branch of a shagbark hickory and chased a rabbit off the lawn. If ever scene was set, this was. All of nature was in tune, and only my stomach a-rumble with nerves was out of it; I didn't know then that a swimmer doesn't *have* to have an empty gut.

The same old deep breath held. Eyes closed (or I would want to stand again), I lay back, trembling, *letting the water fill my ears,* and checked the gasp I made at the rustling thump of it inside my skull. Already a phantom hand was urging the small of my back upward, or at least away. Both arms, at first held taut as if to clutch a non-existent pair of rails, made a forward scoop, shooing squirrels or birds about their business, and took me off balance backward, making my legs lift (*my legs lift!*) from the toehold clutch that moored me like a baby's fingers to its mother. I did a muscular swoon, touching nothing but water, and then brought both arms back to swing them forward again, feeling the water's mass fight back even as I seemed to hover, canted shallowly with lips still high and feet only a foot from home. Everything seemed to unfold, to halt, and it was like being smothered in undulating laundry. The water in my ears made a steady uncorking sound, and somewhere in the deepest water giants were blowing bubbles with cast-iron mouths. My feet hovered like wet cardboard. I felt enclosed, wrapped in surface tension, in whose off-lifted net I was being towed like a drogue parachute target behind a plane. Then I began a mild spiral leftward, corrected it with the merest cuff of my open hand, and began to dip to the right until, with breath still held but aching solidly, I heaved straight again, let out a gasp, and began to go down, slow as molasses out of doors in winter. Foot dipped, I found no floor, so horizontal was I, and without thinking about it I propelled myself backward with a big double lunge which made my drooping feet graze the bottom and then recoil as if it were red-hot.

And they recoiled upward, cut loose, wanting to be free again, to fin-flap, flutter, or trail; but not far enough, so I kept on going down although in semi-swimming position, with breath held on empty lungs, my mind not on this at all but recalling how a sluggish twin-engined plane changed from diving attitude to a climbing one, yet kept on going down while its nose stayed pointed up. Inertia then, inertia now, I thought: I am my own twin-engined blunderbuss; I have no second wind. I have just blundered into how not to sink, as easily as that. Am I dead? Can I do it again before I drown? What did I do? Why was no one here to see? *I can swim.*

It wasn't true; but that three-second levitation had turned my limbs to gold, the water to cumulus clouds the consistency of glue. I had my own Dead Sea. I had found the only coffin-sized chunk of water in the world which didn't let me down. Not even Frankenstein's synthetic man, locked for ages in his wedge of ice (until the Wolfman found him), had felt so much at home in what enclosed him. I looked at water with a different eye. The holy of holies had let me in, after thirty-odd years of trying, and yet nothing in my body had changed. Then I couldn't think at all; my mind quivered, rocked, spasmed, and all its cobwebs blew away into the trees. The bull was in the blue, waiting for me to charge.

Back in lip depth, which I supposed the only place where the miracle might repeat itself, I swung legs up, head back, arms out with dislocation force, and missed the trim that might have made me float. In effect, I had abandoned myself to a backward dive, rather like an outside loop, and I had no idea which way was up, nor enough gumption to twist into a stroke. Panicking once again, I gulped chlorine and thrashed wildly with all limbs until I remembered how to stand. Yet the next time, with a casual slow dither born of spent elation, I crammed my lungs and just lay back on the slanted bunker that was water. There it was, right under me, all of it, and grossly firm. My face went under. Never mind. My toes edged up and broke the surface. My arms began to talk the lingo of the water, discovering how to engulf huge armloads of it and hump them in front of me like bags of fresh-made dough. Then I lay quite still, testing the water's good will, with eyes closed tight and ears given over to the clanking hiss of anesthesia remembered from an operation on my broken arm. I neither sank nor moved, but, still as the sperm pearl on a lily's pistil, waited for the world to turn, looked up sore-eyed at the uninfected blue air and let my breath move into it, expecting to go abruptly down, whereas I went about two millimeters below my private Plimsoll Line. When you'd waited more than half your life for a piece of physics as intimate and ravishing as this, you felt intolerably special even if only for half an hour. And still afloat while able to think about floating. Perhaps, I thought, the mid-life male virgin, flowering at last, knew the same sensation in his new love-maker's high which, once had, he never could undo. My own version was that, after a whole series of suicide squeeze plays, I'd found a creamy equipoise I'd never forget, even if I forgot how to float only an hour later.

Legend reversed itself now as all my previous life began to flash before me. The horn of plenty came to a point beyond the point it used to have, as if it had abstractly been there all along, "produced" as the geometricians say along two dotted lines which used to mean invisible and only in the never-never met. Pulling several g's had never felt this good, or hitting a ball clean over the bleachers out of the park. Or even first sampling the South Atlantic during torrid August. I stood there in mid-pool as if in Xanadu, an exterrorist of myself, aghast at having joined *le water,* and through it the human race, and all those able-bodied swimmers near and dear to me, to whom I'd become a lost cause, a locomoting antique, a teddy bear of lead.

Yet needles lowered onto water had done no less. Frog spawn floated at least as well as I. And now a tadpole I would be, once I'd got the hang of it and learned to harness my dream come true. Everything that twisted vision gave me vanished as I stuck my head back, with bloated certainty cocked my legs even as my altered balance eased them high, and tried to hand-paddle backward from the past into the present. I didn't have to try. With water churning in my ears as if the whole pool had begun to talk, I moved along the surface in a new fit of cardiac excitability: a Viking longboat, an Ojibway canoe, a manatee in love. For some reason, once my head was down, and my ears were full, the whole thing was easy. I ogled my toes, I paddled with my middle fingers only, I aligned my arms with my trunk and splashed my feet with what became a water scansion of smug flourishes that sailed me backward at discernible speed. Back in the half-deep, and spurning all experiment within an arm's reach of the sides, I did it again

and again, with nibbling hands and fluttering toes, and still
had breath enough to sing a raucous hymn of thanks to the
big blue god of wet: improvised doggerel whose banality
revealed my naked joy.

> I float, a boat, I float.
> I even swim, and so this hymn.

It was not immortal, but *I* was, now with a blown-off bloom
of red geranium popped between my toes: a gage, a scalp.

Since no one had arrived to witness this athletic miracle
called flotation, or hear my water music, I began to chant
again, halfway down the pool, touring lazily over the surface, head so far back I floated under a high cabaña of trees,
and when I shut my eyes it was all a squelchy underworld
of mild adjustments, a water-mirth of scale-playing toes,
and hands cupping the water as if they'd found its breasts. I
murmured, with vertically aimed mouth, the only bit of
Greek I could recall, rusty as pig iron, which begins Book
Six of *The Odyssey.*

There he is, good old long-suffering Odysseus, quite
pooped from his exertions, fast asleep, his back encrusted
with salt of the sea, his hair full of briny scurf. When he
wakes, he sees the lovely Nausicaa and her maids, but
scares them half to death by advancing upon them, a
lionlike figure with a leafy twig held over his naked man-
hood, whether or not to conceal an erection I have never
been sure. Taking an unHomeric liberty, I let my mind redo
Odysseus, making him loom up at the girls with penis at the
present arms like Egon Schiele's in his "Self-Portrait Mastur-
bating," with index finger down firm around the root to
tighten the scrotum, or hold the yield back like a rubber
band, and with an unfleshy thumb slap-bang on the tip. I
saw Odysseus guiding his meat.

But it wasn't Odysseus only. How *Roman* swimming felt.
I remembered the baths, the Roman love of pools, the pools

in the houses, the erotic poetry of bathing orgies, and the
Latin for swimming pool, *piscina,* which had all kinds of i's
in it.

> Down in the old piscina,
> Where chlorine shrinks your wiener,
> It's even obscener
> And not much trouble
> To fold it double
> And tuck it in your vagina.

Thus my first ode to the piscina. But, I thought, it wasn't
obscene at all: It was the most decent thing around. There
opened up a whole vista of pleasure in which, now, when
told rudely to go and perform an anatomical impossibility,
you opened your limbs and went and came both ways, with
lubricious calm. Ancient Rome had me by the short hairs
and wouldn't let go.

Uproarious, long, and lewd, that first hour of the float was
a Roman ode of mental abandon, full of calls and cries and
succulent whispers, as if the *pool* were horny. I had never
dreamed it would be so. My stomach had smoothed out for
the first time in years. I wondered if women ever thought of
themselves as having an organ they could, as it were take
out and *do* something to somebody with. Of course. Water
had told me something about woman: not enough, you can
never know enough, but a big, vicarious bonus. The sense of
sex had amplified, triggered maybe by the whoosh-whoosh
that being underwater had in common with the womb. You
fall asleep, lulled by that baby churn, and all your dreams
are wet. The floater becomes the other partner. This male
did, at any rate, and the going rate was low. Just slide in,
and you'll be slid into.

How I came to swim, graduating from spawn to tadpole,
demands feats of memory beyond my league; I no longer
know how not to do it, and it's hard to recall in the right

order the exact overtures to a reflex motion, but I try, I keep
on trying, reconstructing the texture of a miracle, and driving the facts into being with any means at hand—rhymes,
ditties, echoes, itches, fidgets, little tads of washroom filth,
bigger drawings from Pompeii and stations south, deep
elongations of the memory that plays harder and harder to
get, voluptuous questions to a dormant self that only a
dream can answer—until at least some of it comes clear, as if
Trelawny kept trying to say how Shelley looked on the bottom of the Arno. Impossible to say, at least in all the flood-
ing detail I'd like to have, but there one day, if not the
next, and worth having because merely to float made me
feel as if, without even trying, I had invented sex and water
and the human body in the round. I remember some of the
tries that led to the moment, but the moment came about of
its own accord, and I had then, as I have now, a dismal
sense of having gone about everything in the wrong way,
making efforts that only impeded me. The result I got was
none of my causing. And this I knew, even as I told myself
within my bubble of premature glee, you'll never die by
water now.

A more sober analysis of what had happened brought several things together. On that particular day, the water had
been warmer than usual. Moral: the belated swimmer
should never try in water less than 85 degrees Fahrenheit.
Water had gone all the way into my ears, making me flinch,
not from the cold of it, but because it was alien, as on bath
night when I was a child. My entire body felt at ease,
soothed and stroked by a liquid not far from blood heat,
and my ears, letting me feel the water in an intimate way as
well as hear its every gurgle, gave me an uncanny sense of
fusion. I was as much water as the water was, and maybe
the stately integrity of upright balance—with both canals
flooded, so to speak—had given way to something horizontal. I had found a new horizon.

To encourage me further, I who was already bloated with encouragement, Diane had made a lovely new habit of leaving drawings on index cards where she used to leave messages when she went off to teach: by the two ladders, pinned to the blue-green carpet on the deck, lodged inside one of the towels or even floating on the seat of the plastic inflatable chaise that toured the pool in gentle aimlessness, pawn of breeze and flow.

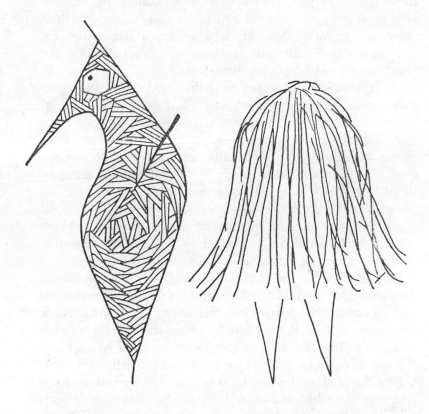

"Armorial Bearings"

There were two kinds, the most endearing a portrait of herself as seen from high up while she slept on her front (as ever) beneath the vast diagonal of her hair, the other tenderly enigmatic: a freehand grackle, pretty well her emblem by now, perched or marooned. The better I became in the water, the bigger the drawings got, as if she gave more of herself each time—both her image and her symbol. I was an aquatic Leander, in several senses, and looking hard at these drawings just before attempting something slightly new gave me extra heart. I reproduce them here for their poise and warmth, their subtlety as armorial bearings for one who, again and again, took on the blue mass in the vinyl trough. My birthday was perpetual. These were its cards, almost always signed with her nickname, Pi, sometimes with the Greek symbol itself. Not only was she enigmatic, as the Muse of the Planets is entitled to be, but she was also my Pilot: she steered, she led, she looked for shoals. So, while I swam and she taught the writing of poetry alongside the tweedy gurus of the nearby campus, there were many imaginary conversations between us, between a Pilot and her *Etwas*. I was an anything that might come to something, as the saying goes, or not—in which event I'd receive a poem, pinned to my trunks, informing me that there were lots of other things to do than swim.

Rolling about in the slop, I was a savage in an Africa; I was all surface, and what was inside me wanted to come out and be surface too, spread like the wings of a manta ray or the waxy perforated caul that butchers strip off the carcass of a sheep. The Masai doesn't know where he leaves off and the earth begins, and when he mutilates himself he is carving up the land, and when he wanders over its surface he is reconnoitering his own skin. In a milder, less urgent form I'd felt something such, especially on days of pure fatigue, when I shaved cheese onto a muffin and saw a strand of my own hair land there too, blown in from foreign parts unknown. Or, because I'd absentmindedly scratched away at some part of my back, I saw spots of dried blood on pillows, sheets, shirts, pajama jackets, and shrugged as if those spots were my spoor, my delegates a little farther away from me than my exhaled breath, the spit that waited to be swallowed or spat. Against the tutored reflex that told me to clean up, indeed to shape up and stop wallowing or stalling amid the detritus of my own being, I heard another voice, another form of excitation, which said there were no boundaries: not between the living me and what I'd shed, nor between living others and what they'd shed too. Human and not-human overlapped so much that the distinction wasn't even worth abolishing. And the temptation to live in filth—not so much a temptation as a gravitation, with earth tugging me down all the time—was merely to come to terms with the tiny veldt of what of me I'd used up and thought I'd left behind.

As the anthropological philosopher Alfonso Lingis says in his essay "Savages," "The body of a savage is so much earth, so much clay, cuneiform tablet. It is not, as ours is for us, the very expression, moment by moment, of an inward soul, or a person belonging to himself."* And the "exorbitant pleasure the savage takes in himself," as Lingis puts it, is a pleasure taken in the land; it is the land, the earth, the soil, that owns both mouth and anus at opposite ends of talkative little tubes called people. This impersonal view of identity came to me via water, of course, as if the space that water filled had reminded me of another space filled with "I," whereas what it was really filled with was slush and sludge, ancient and anonymous. Water abolished privacy along with the notion of the private part, and I remembered a character from an early novel of mine, Alley Jaggers, who

---

* *Semiotext*, III.2, 1978, pp. 96–112. In its original uncut version the essay is even more cogent, and I am grateful to its author for a chance to study it.

at some point, after his model sailplane crashes and he accidentally murders his girlfriend, divines that he was born
only to be a conduit for what he eats. Not so bad, after all?
And for me, the floater, the water that entered my bodily
gaps was doing pretty much what Lingis specifies about
finger, tongue, or penis: not making contact with something
other than surface, but only sliding in "into more surface
effects." We nuzzle one another's inner casings. We are
Klein bottles, whose entrances are their exits. Or Moebius
strips, whose insides are their outsides. Fellow travelers of
our dark and undifferentiated flows, we have a swimming or
a swimmingness within us; indeed, the very concept "within
us" is faint and temporary because what we take into us of
air, water, earth suffers a sea-change during its brief parabola through us and returns to the endless fund. Ingesting or
incorporating, we pretend to host the world, but instead are
only another of the loops through which it goes on its way
to nowhere until the sun bloats and makes of all of us a uniform ash.

Water had brought out the cannibal in me. The water
ahead of me was water I'd already used. The air I breathed
had been recycled for my use. The food I ate did not belong
to me. I was a planet with organs on a planet that had none,
except by proxy. And that swimmingness in me echoed
what I swam in, teaching me that I was only the merest obstacle in between: a membrane, a sheath, a curd on top of
an onion soup. I was in the minority. It was I who'd rupture, snap, or leak, and not the fluids on either side of the
barrier. Water had graffitoed itself all over me, through and
through, heedless of whoever I thought I was, or what.
These recognitions—literally, these *re*-cognitions—came and
went depending on my mood, the degree of my fatigue, the
number of mistakes I made; but they never quite settled
below my mental horizon, and my body got their message

all the time. As in yoga, I became amorphous, and assumed the shapes of other beings.

When the sense of orgy waned somewhat, I still had to convert my free float into the act called swim. Part of me wanted to go on lolling about on the surface with a flower between my toes, and part wanted to cleave the water like a speedboat. What I didn't know was that from float to a crude backstroke was nothing at all, whereas I have never learned the backstroke proper and the breaststroke took three years, and I still can't get the leg part right. Perhaps, because I'd taught myself (or at least floating had come upon me unawares), I didn't heed the formulas that guaranteed success, intent instead on swimming with minimum finesse and maximum fun: a homemade, Rube Goldberg cultist who just frolicked about as if doing something forbidden. Maybe to acquire technique was to rob swimming of its raw magic. Anyway, stuck at a point just this side of drowning, I reckoned it enough, as if I had arrived in heaven and, being there at last, could stay in the Bronx forever and give Fifth Avenue a miss. Able friends of all shapes and sizes egged me on toward perfection, but I resisted: I didn't like to use alternate arms while backstroking, and the breaststroke put my face too near the water for too long. My phobias hung around to hold me back.

I have never advanced much beyond that hot, climactic afternoon of awkward rapture, when I seemed to find that God was kind and could be bought. With infantile gusto I boosted my cupped-hand motions into full-bodied sweeps that shunted me backward for yards behind the prow of my head. I couldn't turn or reverse or tread, but I soon learned I could lift my face and still remain afloat, like sitting up in bed. Bolder than bright at this, I waded to lip depth and then, daring myself to do it, tiptoed until my nose was under and the floor of the pool slanted away down. Out of my depth, I marveled at my lack of fear, staying passive as long as possible to savor the feel of suspended wallow, offering my body to the depths only to cheat them at the last with a back flop worthy of the dentist's chair. Legs up, palms heaving at the water mass, I sprawled backward to safety with head insolently upped. I had come a light-year in an hour. Again and again, I trod on the lip of the deep, tiptoed off it and, in my mind's eye, like a dancer poised at the top of an entrechat, swam back to the shallow end, where in paroxysms of water fever I jumped up and down, slapped the surface hard, rolled and heaved and cavorted and twirled until, too dizzy to stand, I slow-sagged sideways and let myself go all the way under.

My first witness arrived to find me afloat halfway along the pool, blithely paddling with my toes and letting my arms trail, a daft grin on my back-flung face, like a sun wasting helium. "What are you *doing?*" she said. It was the voice of jubilant alarm.

"Just," I said, having waited tens of years to say it, "having a bit of a swim, see. For the exercise." But I was out of breath and my bladder hummed.

"How does it feel?" Her laugh fed on itself, rippling.

"Oh, *voluminous.*" I could have chosen worse words.

"Is that *all?* Keep your head down low."

"Well," I gasped, "a bit—inflated, kind of stranded. I'm going nowhere, but I don't mind."

"Can you remember how it used to feel? That's right, you can move about, you won't lose your balance, the water is holding you up."

"Of course I can. It's like lying on silk, a puddle of silk." But what was underneath it? A slab of slop.

"To qualify, you have to float for two hours—or was it half an hour. But you don't want to qualify, you just want to laze around."

"That's right. This will do for a lifetime."

"I'm *so* proud of you! Now you'll be able to go on and do everything." She motioned up and down the pool.

I said I'd be happy just to lie there and drone songs into the afternoon air. "Hums ancient and modern."

"Dip a leg now and just feel the water stir. You won't fall." With elegant briskness, she mimed it.

"No." I saw Icarus toppling sodden, eyes eggshell blank.

"An arm, then. You'll be quite O.K." More miming.

I was afraid I'd lose my frail water-spider grip on the meniscus. I said no. She went to fetch the camera, and I at once got nervous. I had earned a cup of coffee at least.

"No, don't get out," came the voice of the superswimmer who'd explained it all in vain for years. "This I have to get." *How* did you do it?" Her pleasure almost made her stammer.

I said it just came to me. Like the Wright Brothers at Kittyhawk. It was like going to Andromeda, like seeing after being blind, like a golden egg wrapped in the golden fleece. It was like watching myself being born, and hearing it, feeling it. I squirmed all slithery. The water bore me. I flowed from Lake Champlain to West Point, from Tower Bridge all around the Isle of Dogs. The swoosh was smooth as the celluloid they make pool balls from. Its smell was radiant. Its wet was etched with others' memories. Its murmur was my liquid silhouette. Light as tinsel, I was a parachutist rising. "I just leaned back," I said, "and felt at home." I gave the water both my ears, I kept thinking, and it was like wearing a stethoscope upon my long-withheld equilibrium. Count Basie was playing single notes down deep: *plink*, pause, *plink*, pause, *plink-plong*. It was as thick as feathers, as graspable as mud. All you had to do was watch your mouth.

I quaffed chlorine ale and sea-salt mead, my name, my century, my place, forgotten; I was simply what I was, an amphibian, destined to lifesave and, one day, high dive my first Two-and-a-Half Gainer, Pike Position, before swimming the Hellespont coated with lard. Then I would become my own hovercraft, no longer swimming but whizzing over the water on a cushion of air, all of my own making.

The voice that worked its way into my rapture, and its aftermath, was not the rough-rubble bass which I half-fancied as the voice of Haitchtuo (said with aspirate H as if fogging a lens about to be polished), old chieftain with eels for eyes and a belly full of noxious dams, but she who'd already asked "How'd you *do* it?," bemused, incredulous, pleased as a keg of punch. I came out of my dream and went on touring around the pool with little finlike flourishes and foot flurries, gobbling for breath and somehow talking upward into the sky.

"That's *floating*, really," she said. "It's very good, very good. You taught yourself. I don't believe it. How are you going to celebrate?" So it was true. I had passed stage one.

Consciousness, that hoax of daylit open eyes, seemed to lapse just then, as if my blood had stopped, and I was the outside supervisor of what would soon become a faint. The back of my head swam away from my face. My skeleton softened and flopped. My feet quit. My hands began to dither. Then the sag began, the suicidal going limp I'd heard about. It must be cramp, but it was something else, the blight that comes with my boon and, no matter how well I'm doing, halts me cold, not with exhaustion, nor with fear, but with something awful, as if the will to live has skipped a beat. Curled on the surface, out of my depth, I just went on floating, not in the dead-man's version which is face down, but in the lotus-eater's lounge-about sprawl. I was relaxed, that's why I didn't sink, whereas the mayflies, gnats, sow bugs, and ants about me were all dead, and the horizontally windmilling bees were trying, so hard, to lift off again. A dragonfly like a rearranged biplane patrolled the surface in fast quadrants, a virtuoso of right-angled turns and sudden dizzy sweeps: my private coast guard, I fancied, in my low-blood-sugar trance. Now I was in the deep end and still drifting on the current from the inlet valve even as my tutor braced herself to jump in and rescue the catatonic tiro who'd just been so full of himself.

"Now come back," she said, more calmly than I could believe, telling me I wasn't in any danger, of course I wasn't. I froze, but the freeze floated on. The temptation to let my leg droop, as if to stand and redirect myself, was overpowering and ludicrously wrong, and only a lop-sided fathead would have felt it. Instead, enveloped in all my old dread of deep water, and with not a single ricochet from my earlier pool erotics, I willed the water to be my friend again, the sky not to vanish in a light blue slop, the faint current not to move me deeper. Blasé over five feet had turned to frantic over six. A braver soul would have gone down, touched bottom, and then shoved back upward with a lissom bend of knees; not I, who didn't know what to do on thus regaining the surface. Held overlong, my breath gushed out and I settled fractionally lower, praying not to old Haitchtuo (the god of triumph only) but to the god of amphibians, who gave you half a chance, and was never quite taken in by the shadow play of hand-sized lozenges that rippled on the pool's floor by day, like stepping stones of light, magnified beyond praise.

In that slow, bureaucratic drift I'd gone only a couple of feet. Afraid to wreck my float, I faced upward only but twisted my eyes leftward to the apprehensive face at the coping. "*Come back*," she commanded, and I tried to shrug the raft of myself crosscurrent, but only splashed a trough into which I sank backward. As time dilated and ecstasy went sour, I shut my eyes, held my breath with devout abandon, and felt no waters come closing over me. Unable

to turn, I slopped hard with my feet, as before, but no
longer with the same bravado, instead making each move
with dour precaution; I had to please to get away with this.
I had to combine strictness with cheek, somehow telling the
pool I trusted it all through. The nub of undiluted dread
behind my navel shrank to pea size. With forced familiarity
I stroked the water's top, while my feet became my paddle
wheel.

Soon I was using lax arms again, bold enough to scoop
water back toward the deep. Old Haitchtuo came back to
life, and into his own, while some other god, Bathos of the
Deep, gave up the chase, almost having had me cold simply
because I had no idea how to turn.

Reprieved to play the fool another day, I clambered out
to slightly scolding new congratulations. Nothing risky
when I was alone, I promised, and I saw that, as far as
water went, I was at much the same stage as when I habit-
ually mispronounced *mother* as *mulver* and *certificate* as
cerstifficate and *chimney* as *chimbley*. From a drawer, my
long-suffering water tutor unearthed a trophy from her
early girlhood and awarded it to me there and then: a small
round badge, a stud put out by the Red Cross, which
proclaimed the bearer a Beginner Swimmer, whereas to
come by it honestly, as a mere child, I'd have had to swim a
breadth, tread as well as float; but I took it for all the years
of bungling aspiration. Tempted to slot it into my navel, I
finally anchored it to the collar of an old button-down shirt,
sure again, as always once I was out of the water, that
Saint-Tropez's Hotel Byblos awaited my pleasure: out from
the wisteria-swathed solarium I'd go, into the Arabian
Nights pool, where underwater music tunes you into the apparition of lovers in the depths—Leda being possessed by
her granite swan under the overhang which is the bar's
floor. To be there where jacket and tie are frowned upon,
and brave the water among the aquanauts, hydrophiles, and

pisciniacs, instead of waiting in vain for an unpeopled pool into which to slither from the children's end, that was the payoff, the hydro in the Shangri La of my delight: able not to drown when I collided with other swimmers; to swim full laps and reverse by doing a vertical U-turn underwater; to dive from the highest platform like Dante doing a downward dawn patrol of Hell. That was homage to Haitchtuo, whose logo—a stile (H) being accosted by a grounded cygnet (2) whom a ball (O) pursued—spelled out my need to get some place, even if as an also-swam. *Swim-swam-swum* I told the mirror as I dried my hair: the strong verb's more varied than the weak—*float-floated-floated*. To dawdle on the water was to be dandled on its knee, and my one-eyed father was once again entering the bathroom to scrub my back, the only touch he allowed himself after I reached fourteen, as sensitive to taboo as he was to military protocol. Little did he know that my sturdy back would one day float upon the waters. One careless afternoon's maneuvering had awakened images from far and wide, of being fathered in a lather, and of complementary opposites—piercing and receiving—which inseparably fused in the full heraldic achievement of a backbone ramrod straight, exactly parallel to the sky-blue shelf beneath. My artificial horizon, that cup of always-level mercury, was real. I was halfway up my beanstalk now.

3. OLD-STYLE BACKSTROKE

To be entitled to be so described, which strictly should not be applied to any art or science or anything human, you must be able to swim in all situations, rest in one way or another, vary your attitudes and fear neither cramp, waves, weeds, nor whirlpools. *The perfect swimmer* must have a good constitution, be accustomed to the water, so as not to fear it however cold, and be ready to undertake the longest journeys and cross the most rapid rivers and streams with presence of mind which enables him to see dangers without concern, and to calculate the means of avoiding them—in fact that coolness and courage which is necessary more than anything else, to surmount every kind of peril.

LE COMTE DE COURTIVRON, 1836

My next float was like writing that has gone well and you wake up fast in order to get back to it, half afraid you've lost it overnight. I woke with hands on the comforter, as if already testing the water, feet in position for the flutter-kick that signed the water with my name. Flat on my back, with the all-night active pool not far away (it skimmed and cleansed itself non-stop), I felt like a candidate for Anglo-Saxon ship burial. My backbone was my skiff. My Beginner Swimmer badge was by me on the bedside table, trinket for a novice. I'd reinvented, Diane explained, the old-style backstroke, as rudimentary as walking, but as precious to me as accidentally discovered penicillin. Adapted float that it was, it was a dangerous waking sleep, enabling me to watch my toes, the sun, the trees, Diane's grin of Byzantine complicity, while I lolled on a plastic dimension whose very fluidity, until only yesterday, filled me with dread. Asphyxia could still be had. Some old water nightmare still gave me the chills. But, in general, the world I woke to was different: I was almost twelve feet tall, as high as the pool was wide, and instead of floating widths I'd done half-lengths instead, although a width over six feet all the way was more of a feat than going from six to three. I yearned to walk again to where the floor fell away, and my toes did a vacant glide before I even gave my body to the water. All dams and lakes and reservoirs were six feet shallower already, or was it twelve? The essential shallowness of swimming—you swim in the top two feet—had still not cut its way into my brain, which still dealt in fish that had no eyes, and dark green mortuary tiles untouched since the pool in question had been filled. All along, I could have been a sunfish, a dolphin, grazing that adored surface with my shoulder blades and as much at home as flotsam.

Already, though full of zeal to continue, I felt the seeds in me of the desire not to improve, not to graduate into being a swimmer. I wanted to repeat my one trick until the seas ran dry. Maybe I suspected that my new-found aquatic serenity wouldn't survive my becoming truly competent, as if I believed that only amateurs have fun. Just before I got back in, on an empty stomach, I felt something in the air was wrong, or something in my mind, like the faint cooked-cauliflower reek that wafts off stale chrysanthemums.

Over the next week I tried to develop my primitive back-stroke into something that looked orthodox, but failed utterly to match my arms to my legs. The big forward lunge, as if to hug, first the water and then myself, I'd really got; I could even do some kind of frog kick while moored to the side of the pool. But putting the two together was beyond me; I seemed to need another brain for the second pair of limbs. When my arms moved, my legs forgot to kick, and vice versa. All my legs would do was a genteel vertical scissors, and every other motion felt awkward, mechanical, and —what counted most—merely useful. I was all chronic prefaces, an eternal beginner, as the badge pinned on my trunks declared, not so much obtuse as spellbound still. Stern comments from my schoolteachers came from the depths: "A boy of ability who does not work hard or concentrate." Ah, those old bats knew! But, back then, French had seemed the magic to pursue, and I had slaved at *that*, whereas to slave at something physical: wasn't that superfluous? I wasn't sure. A joy so heavily and hauntedly postponed becomes a spectral image and soars out of its usual category. My mother has always wanted to see Greece, but the prospect of going pleases her more than Greece ever could, so she puts it off until next year, by which time her mental

aked into a snowdrift, so resorting, as Byron pic-
y says, to the "concubine of snow." I myself, I
was resorting to the concubine of water, to soothe
to get again that old anonymous tweak I'd never
was there. Wobbly water felt creational, something
n fog and plasticine. Afloat was more of a halfway
between soil and star than, say, being buried, or wav-
breakfast tray to feel the cushion of air build up in
of it. Flat-topped and homogeneous, water was more
y intuited as one thing than a garden or an atmosphere,
ost akin to being inside a tree, a root of celery, or a
shroom cap. And *I* was the element in which the *water*
am, urged gently from inlet valve to the gentle skimmer
irty feet eastward, the half of the water that got the eve-
ing sun only, because tall shagbark hickories shaded it.
When I floated low, insects landed on me as if I were water.
Sun bronzed my face while chlorine bleached my back. In a
dwindling declension of impostures, I was a crocodile, a log,
a bark canoe, a cast-off grass skirt, sargasso gulfweed, a
cloud of seed fluff from the quaking aspens, then plankton
skimmed into the plastic basket behind its tossing plastic
flap.

If my sex life improved with what became my awkward
daily swim, I have yet to be told. I became no fitter, no
firmer, no smarter, but I had somewhere new to go, which
was mighty important: a skin-tight Eden in which to mess
around, dreaming berserk or Blake-like dreams while floating backward from the deep end's ghastly doorway. Always
moving away from it, I mentally said a thousand *close it,
sesames* to the door whose name's the name of an oily seed,
a laxative in fact, and I wondered if the whole of *The
Arabian Nights* might just be covert constipation. Sesame
opens if you take enough, and the door (at least as I
remember it) is the same shape as the seed, so the argu-
ment may hold, whereas the door to my unsampled deep,

buildup's even bigger,
for gain but to be kept,
of honor, next to a preciou

So too with me. No wat
I swam two ways: in water,
my head, where I always we
and did all strokes for some
baby, stooging around the tu
remembered Peter Pan and revel
of obligation to care, to move, t
never be among those athletes of pu
parade ground, my oasis, their gymna
worked while I achieved a swim-still
the interface of water and air.

The whole puritanism of doing as one
joying something more than bimbos deer
gone past me long ago when, eager for th
senses, I'd found out my inability to like son
manner laid down. Commanded to "study" A. \
Eothen ("Toward the East") for examination
sank toward it gamely, reveling in the camels, th
saries, the unforgettable image of the haughty Lad
Stanhope, eccentric aristocrat riding her camel
broomstick. What all this "meant," I had no idea, and
don't see why life, so long as we have it, should be "m
ingful." We are here to bring our apparatus to bear, to
up a mostly vanishing quota, say "thanks for the nice time
and go, which is why it seems to me worthwhile doing nothing more inventive than feeling my blood run, my eyes
blink, my muscles twitch, all of these minima vaster than
the nothing we go toward. We underestimate the delicious
nullity of how things feel, in the body, when they're going
right, as my father found.

In a note appended to *Don Juan,* Byron reminds us how
St. Francis, "inflamed with a wonderful fervor of the mind,"

plunged
turesque
guessed,
myself,
known
betwee
house
ing a
front
easi
alm
m
sv
tl

although no doubt the same shape as a cross-section of the pool, was universe-wide and many-shaped, as easily the Coalsack in the Southern Milky Way as the intersected arcs we drew with carnal pairs of compasses (their needles in the nipples or the knees), and watercolored idyll-pink or realist-brown, a long time ago, in school, before I even realized I'd been born.

Perhaps the introverted boy I'd been had early realized, peering at graffiti in the back of his geography book, that as much of us as of the rest of the world is water. We might easily pour away, fade into the dew that scared the young Hamlet. If in the end only bone prevailed, surviving as what I called "skelingtons," everything else went down the drain. I'd tapped the vein of insecurity, from the fillable to the spongy, from the porous to the spinal. We were no more real than powdered potato. After all, Hamlet isn't holding Yorick's liver or his heart when he utters that profoundly affecting and all-inclusive *Alas:* the ducts, the valves, the filters, and the swellables have gone back into the planet, are once again one with nature; the rabble of his lubricants has scattered, never to recombine as Yorick anyway. No wonder it's these—our sticky stuffs—that prompt disgust in folk who think we should have cuckoo clocks within, whereas bone (just listen to that word) demands an almost puritanical esteem because it's—well, not messy.

In this sense, then, to immerse yourself is to flirt with the last, fatal draining away. Like hearties who commit a bit of mutual suicide every time they kill a bottle together, we die a bit when we dunk ourselves into a bigger slop than our little sphincters contain. Bottles in the ocean indeed, we pride ourselves on being sealed vessels who amiably ride a flux that came from lightning roaring into water. Tugged by the osmosis that never has to woo its electorate, we swim in unwitting rehearsal, doomed to vary incessantly the few figure-ground combinations of the human antic: the minor

ruffling the main in a mood of bemused comparison, in a
single splash having it all ways: back to the origin of life;
back to Mamma; and forward, in a hectic second-guess we
hardly know we make. When the swimmer works, that
echoes life and the daily grind. When the swimmer floats,
that's an assent to our mortality. And when a beginner-
swimmer floats, with not much hope or aim of doing more,
that's bone-idle pessimism.

How well we know this racial tic, not only running fau-
cets to tease the bladder on, ascribing hemorrhages and
madness to the moon, loosening our sinuses with basins of
steam or (by accident) steaming soup, but also resorting to
the *tulchan,* for instance, which is a calfskin stuffed with
straw, set beside a cow at milking time to boost the udder's
flow. Some of us sleep beside recordings of rain or white-
noise surf. Even a color postcard of the pool at a certain
hotel in Key West works for me, and I entrance myself with
that big blue oval in which to float is to drift along God's eye.
Somewhere between witchcraft and biological feedback, we
prod ourselves uncommonly well, advancing from likeness
and the bit-that-represents-the-part to outright symbolism.
Maybe we think our images are strong, as if to say, we can
imagine ourselves into any state, which suggests that reality
is largely mental—as, for the physicist trying to measure
electrons, it is. You can't describe them without describing
the experiment in which you are trying to pin them down.
Between electrons and electron-watchers' minds, there's no
perfect separation. Perhaps brute matter apes our metaphors after all, then; or, to put it in another way, if, as an astounding number of people believe on the basis of no evidence at all, a sentient entity oversees us, it will at long last
inform itself: *So this is what they want; heaven knows why,
but they do.*

No wonder, in a universe like this, I stuck at the nursery
stage in swimming for two whole years, neither forgetting

nor moving on, engrossed in genuine false starts that mixed up death with what was lewd. At least I got my boyhood back, and the joy, the weight, of that slowed me down no end. It was a boyhood in which, now, I swam, in both senses, and after a month or so I remembered something left in the chimney of a house we'd left behind: up past the fireplace, on the right-hand ledge inside the bottom of the chimney, I'd concealed half a dozen enormous jars of copper sulfate solution, sealed with grease-proof paper held by rubber bands, against what exact emergency I wasn't sure—perhaps a swimming pool of my own, which I'd fill once the hole was dug. There in the dark, improbably warmed by some invalid's bedroom fire, the jars still sat, undisturbed after thirty-odd years, with just a little patina of dust and muck upon them, reconnoitered by frustrated mice. Whoever found them held them up to the light, I hoped, before pouring them away or chucking them out unopened, and so saw the azure coming through, the sheer bulk of the celestial in the H_2O. Both death and ecstasy, I realized, evicted you from yourself, and surely anyone who wants to live intensely tinkers with both, much as, on a completely different level of palpable shamelessness, the three strapping Honeybone sisters, Ella, Bella, and Della, in the village of my childhood, diced with rape: three coal-haired Amazons who Vaselined their pubic beards downward and so wore no underwear when they strode out in perfect step, on stiletto heels, on Sundays. Three birds of prey they were, ravening to be preyed upon; but only one was strangled, although one of the other two died young.

I doodled with infinity, reluctant to carve my will into the water because learning to "go"—to surrender body and soul —seemed more important than learning safety first. An odd and doltish view, no doubt, it worked its way through me, accomplished itself in full, then sealed itself away like a condolence envelope. One day, after dawdling about for an

hour in my habitual slow motion, I recovered my desire to
swim and, tight-assed as a brand-new convict, turned left,
shoved off into a terrifying forward float and parted the
inside-out prayer of my hands into the crudest breaststroke
ever done. My legs went down, but I blunder-floundered to
the side of the pool, cheered on by my tutor, in four or five
gross flopping motions that filled my mouth with water and
told me I'd made an irrevocable stride. I had asserted myself, shuddering to have my face so near that flood, yet in
another state of mind as well, borrowed from the five-inch
frontiersman given me in my tenth year to install inside my
fort and defend it to the death: prone on his elbows with
hands clasped around his flintlock rifle, and a bandolier over
his shoulder. In much that pose I "breasted the main,"
smirking a little as I said the antique phrase aloud.

With auspices and goals made clear, I almost shed rapture for athleticism, making myself pull both arms way past
my hips during the stroke, and forcing them down deep to
move a lot of water. Slaphappy cockleshell, bobbing about
on the sclera of Creation itself, I tried to breathe on the
backward shove. Did I dream it, or had my new abandon
created chemicals in me that gave me better rhythm, in
which dogged repetition (*"Peel* your hands apart. Bring
them back close to your sides. Loop them under your arm-
pits.") actually worked? It was like gaining speed without
leaving Archimedes behind. Brain chemistry and specific
gravity came together. Everything I needed was at hand,
had I only the brains to use it, and there were patterns built
into nature that even I, within my beginner's limits, could
learn to use. How *did* parasitic wasps know where the wasp
eggs they exploited—eggs of other kinds of wasps—were exactly on the inside of a fig, down in the jungles of Belize?
The known kept returning me to harmony, symmetry, the
quality in nature I'd begun to call *provided-for,* and so to
beauty, the term I'd tried to leave behind. The vision of in-

genuity—not just of the clockwork hen that laid a wooden egg, not just of the astounding way in which the breast-stroke worked, but of things' interrelatedness—woke me up. Call it the delicate unprecedentedness of all there was. Call it the is-ness as distinct from all the imaginable things that did not exist in nature. I preferred jaguars to peccaries, lilies to dandelions, cardinals to crows, but only on the level of habit. On another level, where I couldn't pick and choose without being a sectarian fathead, I had to take into account all things bright and beautiful *and* all things their exact opposite. The fancy word for this was "entelechy," which meant not only something's is-ness, but how its is-ness had evolved and was evolving, which included the thing's capacity to achieve itself along a certain time line, either perfect (the roach, say, unchanged since the Age of Coal) or still in train (the fishes of Bikini atoll in the trees). To what extent, you asked the roach, those fish, have you fulfilled your promise? As for such flukes as waltzing mice, top-heavy turtles, the monstrous antlers of the Irish elk, the arthropod's brain blocking its own alimentary canal, or the marsupial brain with its hemispheres inadequately con-nected, these were the by-blows of an evolution that kept on puzzling its way through, to whatever imaginable termi-nus. As Leo Rosten said, "If you don't know where the road goes to, it sure as hell will take you there." And what in-trigued me was the steady force behind it. I myself, shifting from float to backstroke to breaststroke, was *evolving*, along the same lines as billions of humans had evolved before me, yet with my own clumsy variations, whose precursors were legion: a voice in the muscle sheath, a twitch in the joints.

I was living out a piece of the natural structure. I was paying a belated call on physics. Here were countless in-teractions of my skin, muscles, and weight with water, un-told little symmetries all behaving themselves. It was like hearing, as one can, the cry of a child in the impeded-

sounding churning of a bulldozer. I called it beautiful, this
role of my body as a tool, suddenly aware that the bother-
some word *esthetic* was nothing but a mutant of old Greek
aisthetes, which meant "One who perceives." The concept
of beauty was never in esthetics anyway, which was why
Plato, when fudging up his famous divided line (rather like
a TV antenna with the form of the Good at the top and
wholesale delusion at the bottom),

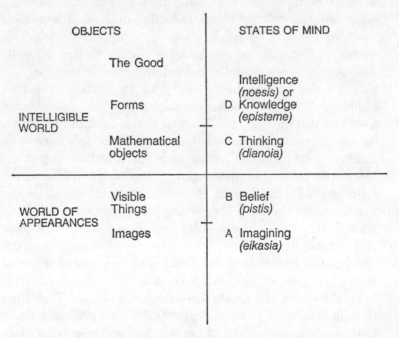

OBJECTS		STATES OF MIND
	The Good	
INTELLIGIBLE WORLD	Forms	D Intelligence *(noesis)* or Knowledge *(episteme)*
	Mathematical objects	C Thinking *(dianoia)*
WORLD OF APPEARANCES	Visible Things	B Belief *(pistis)*
	Images	A Imagining *(eikasia)*

had to invent words of his own for various mental states and
what they contained. Or he twisted the drift of words he already had. Imagine sticking the perceived in place of the
beautiful; I almost drowned, laughing at my effrontery.
Plato wanted the good or the beautiful where the Greeks already had the perceived and the perceivable. All things
bright and perceived, I sang, behind my swimming tutor's

back; *Black Perceived* (a horse), *The Testament of the Perceived* (a long poem no longer by Robert Bridges), *Seven Perceiveds* (a movie). Over and above taste and preference, there was a democracy of the perceived, and all perceivables were blessed. They were endowed with being whether they were alive or not, *onts* if not *bionts*, entities if not organisms. One day, conceivably, art as such would end, or lapse into an ancillary role, and its only esthetics would be to reproduce in this or that medium the handiwork of Creation. There would be the as-is, tinted in various ways but durably recognizable, and deliberate distortions of this norm. All perceivedness would refer to what was there to be perceived, or to recognizable departures from it. Art would simply draw attention to the physical universe, much like the Nobel laureate down the road from where I write these words, an astrophysicist who, during a train journey in the late Thirties from Washington, D.C., to Ithaca, New York (when Ithaca had trains), doodled on the back of an envelope and in that short spell, for all time, figured out how stars bigger than our own sun work (the carbon-nitrogen cycle). Only a year earlier he had guess-reasoned that the sun, and similar stars, use another process known as proton-proton reaction in order to turn *their* hydrogen into helium. The astonishing thing is that Hans Bethe was able to divine which two, of the many ways to convert hydrogen into helium, were of special importance for stars. The universe had won his attention and he had imagined his way into its furnaces.

Aisth, I lisped into the water's brim, it means *here to know*, including a whole underworld of underprized phenomena: the peccary, dandelion, crow, why the very pancreas itself, not in some Little League order of beauts but as a helping of equal *aisth*. Taste had no bearing on the universe itself, whose stylistics are less free than ours, having come out of sheer survival as a living form. A long emer-

gency was behind that art, if art it was, of peccary and all
the rest, the human brain included, and so-called wobbles
in the genetic code were the marks of its birth. One day
soon, I told myself, breaststroking from one side to the
other, when the joys of prowess have ousted all your rever-
ence for water, your uneasiness with the word beauty will
go, and you'll see that the universe doesn't always produce
winners any more than Cézanne, Nabokov, or Villa-Lobos
did. You are trying to reduce the spectrum of the created to
a single hue, just in order to pay tribute more conveniently.
You don't have to lump everything together just because the
world of the electron microscope remains largely unenjoyed.
The magical is not necessarily a joy to the eye, the nose, the
ear: some amino acids revealed by that microscope are prettier than others, never mind how cleverly the others are
stained. Stop trying to homogenize.

Half-losing that dialogue with myself, I wondered why
the notion of beauty struck me as so much bigotry when, in
most unguarded moments, I'd prefer flame tree to oak, Bal
à Versailles to Chanel any number, and any perfume
known to the body odors of Jean Genet, which Genet in jail
voluptuously inhaled under a blanket, a desperate nosegay
to himself. Instead of floundering around in the water, like
one who'd never learned, I wanted to execute the swimming
equivalent of the gymnast's "straight tsukahara," an aquatic
loop-the-loop, even if my own version came out, as the experts say, "slightly dished." Yet a part of me was willing to
go on, reverentially muddling around, arriving at felicities
only by accident (maybe like evolution itself). I wanted it
both ways, trying within one body, one head, to undergo
Creation at its worst and best, cancer cell and leprosy,
phagocyte and lymph, in one. It wouldn't work, of course:
even *my* swimming would improve unless, in a prolonged fit
of perversity, I went all out to make it bad, thus edging it
over from what was uncouth and ungainly and ugly (it

worked but was no prettier than my pancreas!) toward what I just couldn't call the perceivable when I meant its neatness, its competence, its trespass on the fish. Finally, I saw, though reluctantly, that the Creator or Evolution has no human parallel and, in dealing with raw chemistry, had less freedom than we accord ourselves with paint or words or musical scales. I knew that biologists had claimed evolution is limitless variations on limited themes and I knew that human thought overall is limited variations on not many themes either.

It sounded like a parallel, but there was, ultimately, only one set of laws by which I swam, whereas there were thousands of ways of describing it in words, in paint, in music. I trusted survival more than I trusted taste; the dinosaur hadn't made it, whereas the awful sonnets of Michelangelo had; if I were Mister Entelechy, I'd have had more trouble devising the dinosaur than in making those sonnets. We humans sounded more restricted, doing less with less, than Mister E., doing an endless amount with not very much, but it wasn't true, and mere opinion didn't enter into the survival of the fittest, whereas survival entered only as a metaphor into the lottery of which works of art survived, a law less harsh than that which rendered certain inventions obsolete. Trying to put my view together, I thought of Carlo Gozzi, author of *Turandot*, who'd said there were only thirty-six tragic situations. Was that a comment on art or life? Or merely an unwitting proof of human narrow-mindedness? The universe expands, the mind gropes after it; and I, awkwardly swimming, into and out of my depth, knew only that a bit of me was verbally free, to marvel and exclaim and make exact, whereas most of me was in the physics trap, which made you sink or swim.

Never had I realized how inexorable the universe could be, compared to the mild freedom of the human mind. By quite a different kind of law from that which let me float, I could take or leave all kinds of artifacts, including even those the scientist rejects. Fit to survive in water (shallow water anyway), I was my own progenitor a bit; but the only life-and-death rule about what went on in my head was that, one day, it would stop. The ugliness and beauty of the universe was a fluke, and I was just another fluke trying to sift the one from the other by quite haphazard standards: Not all dangerous things looked awful or smelled bad. I'd end up swimming well, just to relieve that mental pain.

Something forlorn, funereal, had been in my awkward swimming from the start. Water was oblivion, a nearby sample of how the universe washes us away, and all water contained—whether I tried to swim in it or not—the death and vanishing of everyone I held dear. If ever a man shortchanged in one coinage (to swim or not) was more than compensated in another (affection), I was that man. I have gone around for days, my head creaking and aching with the amount of affection I get, who least deserve it, and with the effort of reconciling anything so ingeniously and up-front generous with the dissolution and death of those givers. *How can consciousness end?* Diane asks repeatedly. *Because the universe doesn't need us,* I answer: *We're all by-blows, gratuitous bonuses. We're expendable.* But no phrase, no series of arguments, even touches the nub of it. The nub of it is non-sense, when all the love and beauty and bravery of the human drain away and become, for a while, elegant figures in some other loser's memory. It has always been in water (not in arid lands or up high) that the basic ludicrousness of being alive comes clear. Maybe even a laundry would do: We speak of being washed out, or washed away; but we are the laundry too, and that entails being in the tub, the vat, the pool, for these are anti-wombs in which this sketchy stuff—two bits of hydrogen to one of oxygen—merely tolerates us, who belong elsewhere. Immersion, then, unlike sunbathing or sleep, is much like dying, because you are already wrapped around in watery winding cloths, and the dreams you have are of the day, deliberate and adroit. Somehow the pool, which you can make your own—swimming all over it year after year until not a drop of the water hasn't slid off your back—wipes out your presence second by second. You leave no trace. Or, as Charles Tomlinson says in his poem "Swimming Chenango Lake," the swimmer

> . . . reaches in-and-through to that space
> The body is heir to, making a where
> In water, a possession to be relinquished
> Willingly at each stroke. The image he has torn
> Flows-to behind him, healing itself. . . .

That's what galls me, that's the rub. The water always regroups as if you've never been, and this makes swimming just about the most refined version of the game called Being Present at Your Own Absence. When you glide forward, you have truly gone beyond yourself, leaving no trace, although the water, like its universe, will let you use it. Against such baleful stuff there are only other games, such as the one Diane and I engage in when my tummy is the Moon and my bunched fist above it a Moon-lander, which then splays it fingers, rocking and swaying until the gentlest touchdown near the navel, after which one forefinger scoops up a contingency sample, and roams the area of soft curvature as a lunar rover. When I raise the thumb of the flag we toot the National Anthem at speed and the whole Lander begins to pulse at the crouch like a space-age crab until, with a foot-high leap, it lifts away to an accompaniment of mentally supplied fireworks and rejoins the command module of my head. It takes about a minute only and can be played while floating in the water, a riff of tender joy repeated indefinitely in the ambit of something that is next to nothing, where the two-faced water mindlessly awaits the swimmer who comes next. And, such is the paradox of my being, that next one is I, saying, almost out of control with longing, *I must get to the sea, I must get to the ocean, I must be near the water, I don't know why.* Is that hunger for the sea a hunger, then, for death? I doubt it; but the death of hunger, gauche as it sounds, it might be that.

We do not hear as much of the Absurd as we used to; in cold storage with Kierkegaard and Camus, the term has lapsed from vogue, but still evokes anything that is *surdus,* meaning irrational or senseless and so, by unkind extension, backward or deaf (*sourd* is "deaf" in French). The Indo-European root, *swer-2,* means to buzz or whisper (whereas *swer-1,* the regular guy, means to talk or speak). Greek *alogos* (= speechless, irrational) gave us *jadhr asamm,* which is Arabic for a deaf root, while one dictionary says the *ab* means "utterly" and another says it means "away from" in the phrase "away from right sound." How the *swer*-word itself buzzes, with things suppressed and locked away, bogeymen and bugaboos. Albert Camus defined it, or perhaps it would be more accurate to say that he bravely refined it, as the gap between minds that yearn and the world that lets them down, by which we usually intend death, or the way our universe looks after itself, heedless of individuals. But to complain that the universe, so to speak, doesn't treat us as well as it does itself is to liken the human to the cosmic, and not that justifiably. Semi-facetious allusions apart (yes a human can be a white dwarf, even a red giant), you and I are quite unlike the universe: not expanding or contracting or pulsating, nor made up of clusters of galaxies strewn throughout a vacuum, nor even as constant as suns, as untidy as an open cluster, or for that, as organized as a molecule, as inscrutably omnivorous as a black hole. Indeed, even where the universe might seem a bit absurd—with its so-called "wobbles" in the genetic code, with six ways of making one essential chemical but only one of making another chemical just as essential—it still gets by, through a predominance of successful chances.

We are not the small version of that; the universe is an absolute, which means it needs nothing but itself, whereas we humans want to be without lack, as Sartre says. You could, I suppose, work out an exact ratio of component parts, likening molecules to hypothetical planets around many, many stars, and human individuals to suns, families to clusters, clans to galaxies; but the universe, made of the same stuff as we, is what includes us, and continually reuses us. We cannot sever ourselves from it to become unobligated exceptions. All we can do is heed what we have in common with suns, as we heed what we have in common with elephants or clouds without becoming elephantine or cloudy, and cease being infatuated with metaphors that take us from the body to the body politic, from a body of thought to bodies celestial. Our special gift, it seems, is to be the universe's way of pondering (and disliking) itself, and that gift brings hazards with it, including disliking the way the universe uses us to formulate a dislike of itself it can ignore without using us at all.

Even worse, if you settle for the human microcosm vis-à-vis the cosmic microcosm, you first of all run into Beckett's nastiest aphorism and get wounded by it: "The mortal microcosm cannot forgive the relative immortality of the macrocosm." The word "relative" evinces our indignant ignorance, but also reminds us that anyone who makes microcosms, and wants them accurate, has to reckon with this: Each microcosm adds itself to the macrocosm (it has nowhere else to go), so an accurate microcosm has to include—in little, of course—all the microcosms that have been added, are being added, will be added to the great big cosm itself. Halt everything, you say; no more microcosms added until mine's finished. Impossible. Just as the expand-

ing edge of the universe outstrips the astronomer's tele-
scopes, so does the constant surfeit of microcosms outstrip
the micro-cosmetician who, in the very act of trying to sum
up, both thwarts himself and renders others obsolete. A less
than tolerant view of how our little versions go astray is
Dylan Thomas's juxtaposition of Llaregub and Llarebyg,
which reverse into "Buggerall" and "Biggerall," in other
words nothing and everything. The universe at large does
funny things. Galaxies collide or deform one another; every
now and then, a subatomic particle called the anti-sigma
minus hyperon goes the wrong way; and, each year, in a putative room full of radium atoms, one dies, but why that
particular one we have no idea. The universe does funny
things within us too, making children age at enormous
speed until a ten-year-old is bald and toothless, or making a
mongol here, a cretin there, or making me inherit from my
mother's side the migraine which must have had a first
sufferer somewhere in the family tree, saddling my sister
with a quarter-sized nevus on her writing hand (a port-
wine plateau of scab that bled), and making my niece a
celiac case, unable to metabolize gluten.

The analogy we need beyond word, simile, metaphor (all
of them analogies) is between the *race* and the universe; although not as old, we and it co-exist, though surely we will
never keep pace, not we humans, afflicted with the primitive old brain that the famous Broca called the limbic system. If, as individuals indignant about the prospects for our
race, we call ourselves absurd, then we have a case of sorts,
and in the main only ourselves to blame. The universe is not
subject to its own conscious will, whereas we are subject to
our own, and it is only the universe's good luck to be so big
we haven't been able to dominate it all, we who should not
ape the violence of the stars themselves but exercise whatever degree of self-control we have, never mind how slight.
Our ironic fate is to be—in the thick of the All—not only

implicated, but conscious, and unable all the same to see that, although the universe includes our race, the universe itself is not included in anything, much as we cannot see that, although the race includes us all, the race is not the same as any individual, is predicated on transcendence, not on soothing parallels. Galileo has it clear in his *Dialogue on the Two Great Systems, Giornata I,* where he says:

> As for those who so exalt incorruptibility, inalterability, I believe they are brought to say these things through their great desire to live a long time and through the terror they have of death. And not considering that, if men were immortal, these men would not have had an opportunity to come into the world. They would deserve to encounter a Medusa's head, which would transform them into statues of jasper or of diamond, to make them more perfect than they are. . . . And there is not the slightest doubt that the Earth is far more perfect, being, as it is, alterable, changeable, than if it were a mass of stone, even if it were a whole diamond, hard and impenetrable.

If you buy that, you relegate the absurd to social or stylistic incongruity, which includes, I suppose, wanting the universe to behave toward us like a caring parent doomed to die before us, and glad that we can carry on the seed, the blood, the unappeasable longing never to vanish, for all eternity, into the uncaring but endlessly receptive chemistry of the cosmic machine. If, as a race, we cared as much about survival as about individuals, we would behave racially better, much as other races on other planets may have been doing for ages, deterred by contempt from communicating with us, even over a distance colossal enough to keep us at bay. *If* the absurd exists, *we* are it.

The pessimism of cosmologist Fred Hoyle, whose delight in the universe does not extend to humankind (breeding

and brawling), sets him apart from those euphoric, high-
energy theorists who rule the roost and look on the bright
side, but somehow never manage to persuade unorganized
humanity to behave any better. That is what's absurd: to
have the inkling without being able to make it count. While
we talk about getting our house in order before the hypothetical time limit ascribed to violent technological societies,
stars evolve and die all the way along the curve of the
Hertzsprung-Russell diagram for star formation, immune
and remote; Nero might just as well be an astronomer,
rather than nothing at all, admiring the heavens while the
matrix of mankind goes up in smoke. Second things put first
can ravish us even in the depths of our shame. The race will
go to the wall, not better, but better informed, which is like
saying a can opener doesn't work but has a lovely shine.

Having breaststroked a maximum of ten yards at a time, I
expected to graduate from a width to an actual length or
lap. But, once again, something began to go wrong. I'd
freeze, especially in the moment before the first stroke
began, and fall from my float. Sometimes my legs weren't
high enough, but most often I just forgot to move them at
all. For at least a year, I towed their dead weight behind
me, unable to move them when I moved my arms. When I
kicked, my arms went dead, and I looked down into the
pale blue vacancy, its prey, yet rejoicing in its tender indul-
gence, its double face. I soared upon it only to become
a water catatonic, murmuring the still-water version of
Byron's

> How many times have I
> Cloven with arm still lustier, breast more daring,
> The wave all roughen'd; with a swimmer's stroke
> Flinging the billows back from my drench'd hair,
> And laughing from my lip the audacious brine. . . .

Hard work in the water raised my level of norepinephrine, the adrenal hormone that in turn raises blood pressure, and I got my amateur swimmer's high that lasted half a day. I swam away my cares, at least until, down on the bottom, I saw the gourd mask of Max Ernst's painting *The Obscure Gods* awaiting me, with snowball eyes and azure beak, hemmed about with shattered-crystal radiants like a monster galaxy imploding. Down there, six feet down, nothing was on the human scale, not even the pale caterpillar the vacuum head had missed, the white leaves, the spreadeagled spider like a specimen mounted in an album. Such matter had a nasty hold upon my mind.

Before becoming the compleat swimmer I almost wished to be, I'd have to twist my way of looking at deep water. I folded the jacket of my pajamas neatly up, then slung the pants awry beside it on the bed. Now, did I still have to fold the pants or dishevel the jacket? Which did I prefer? I left each as it was, unable to decide. I wanted to reach the aquatic equivalent of looking at a single word until it no longer registered meaningfully, so that I no longer knew which depth cracked your skull if you dived into it or offered the beginner swimmer a blue meadow in which to graze. Unable to tell shallow from deep, or up from down, I'd have no bearings at all, no beefs, no dreads, no dreams. I'd be the zero-gravity student-pilot in his hooded cabin, blind-swimming much as he blind-flew. Still a landlubber at heart, I stood on the bottom and dived upward by shoving down. I lay on the bottom with flinching open eyes and made myself dread the water above me instead of yearning for it as the safety zone. That helped a bit. I floundered underwater from six feet, up to the shallow end, all the time rehearsing a similar journey to the diving board, and telling myself that, in water, all journeys were the same. No good. Mind over matter was sorcery-bright, but mind over mind was no good at all. Depth and mass and volume came to-

gether, a universe too big for me, and it was only a year
later that I managed the breaststroke complete, whispering
forward and *back* as, at long last, I learned to use my arms
and legs alternately, with always an extra-heavy heave at
the shoulders to make up for my legs' refusals. Floating had
felt like cheating, but the breaststroke felt like work, even
as I sensed the joys: cobbled undulations of the water
against my stomach that became an undertow against the
top of my feet. Did people ever tire of this? Was there ever
a day when the swimmer came up with nothing new? When
the thrill had gone? Doomed to a perpetual water puberty,
I'd never know, I'd not lived long enough to be any good,
I'd never outlive the thrill. Instead, while thrilled, I went on
with my swimming task; the faces of my worn-out grand-
mothers came to me as, each day of their lives, with looks of
intent, forbearing exasperation, they attacked the chores of
the hearth, scooping out ashes, twisting firelighters from
rolled-up newspapers, black-leading the clanging fire irons,
until the shrine of soot was right. Each time the face implied that life could be richer than this, certainly better
than facing into the grimy back of the fireplace as if expecting Santa Claus in mourning to descend the chimney.

Water was lovelier by far than soot (or was that preju-
dice?). Yet I stared at it with their same sense of helpless
obligation, always having to grapple with it, and unable to
see a way out. I often almost wished I hadn't started, knowing that swimmable water lay in wait for me all over the
planet. My limited skill I could actually transfer; and, after
a while, I became a sampler of pools and oceans, never rising to the dramatic plunge, but slithering truantly in, a connoisseur of slop channels, a maven of the exact hue of blue,
a savorer of water temperature, chlorinity, gradient, and
above all how the sun at different heights and angles
changed the lozenge pattern on the bottom, where skewed
oblongs bent and swirled, overlapped and spun like pucks

of denuded copper-sulfate light that wafted lazily toward a swimmer's legs. When actually afloat, I looked down into the supple sway that held me, thrilled by its seamlessness, but always waiting to fall through it into Haitchtuo's pink maw. Haitchtuo was also Goya's Saturn, I'm afraid, who chomps that son of his head first.

Pool blue was never in the sea except in the Bahamas, where certain shallows lure you with a duck-egg green in which to swim is to enter one of Cocteau's fluid mirrors. I felt an enormous relief at swimming over a bottom so far out-of-reach it didn't matter; but the waves fouled up my rhythm and I didn't foul up theirs. The foreshortened vastness all the way to the horizon made me feel like a true island, and a floating one at that, which no longer tilted clawing between panic and vertigo. Lie back and let your ears fill up, I told myself. Heave away and trust it. I did, and the sea dropped out of my textbook of horrors.

Yet, shifting from whatever I did on my back to what I did on my front entailed moving through two right angles, after the first of which my legs took me down almost every time. I couldn't tread. Legs bent, knees high, torso crouched, arms and hands just cupping and tootling near the top somewhere, I did my braille of basic moves and sank. Some folk suffered from big bottom or were just too buoyant, but I had no more symmetry than a mess of plankton; like one of those picturesque plum puddings cooked up by the astronomers, that swell to show us what the universe is like, I had no center, no point of reference. I was a blob, an infestation of myself; but a summer season later, after a winter of almost no swimming at all, I attempted a backward-leaning angle I was sure no other human had used, and with my feet almost horizontal found the magic point I could rotate about, then spent long hours trying to save myself with it while swinging from float to breaststroke. The worst moment was the shift from tread to prone, when I felt

altogether at the water's mercy, and the creases in my
trunks unfolded to admit freshets of cold. Then I chinned
the water and struck out for all I was worth. After a while, I
could rear back from breast- to backstroke with a delirious
showy twist that betrayed how safe I felt to be on my back
again. And, when I came to advance into deep water in my
converted tread (stand-up advance at an inch a minute), I
knew that only water could soothe the strain in me that
swimming caused. I played into the water's hands, and people came to watch this freak, this floating unicorn who did
in an inhuman way what people took for granted.

On the very best day, under a scorching sun and in water
bath-water warm, something new happened right in the
middle of an awkward maneuver I'd just begun to be
ashamed of making. All of a sudden I felt as if I too were
made of water, able to spin and pirouette, and carelessly
roll upside down, not just buoyant but water-motivated,
water-inspired: a puppy who switched strokes by means of
a simple twist and, to show himself the dread had gone, did
his twist repeatedly, daring the water to let him down. But
no: that uniform smothery sheath bent and stretched with
me like the tissue paper around the conjuror's twisted ciga-
rette. I felt serpentine, all coils and swirls, as legless as
armless, and I seemed to flow quite unpropelled, squirming
blasé for hours on end till even those who most genuinely
applauded the miracle grew weary and retreated with a
nod. I made a circuit of the pool, closely watched by my
tutor, who had written three books while I learned how to
swim, but I soon resumed my free cavort in the semi-
depths, certain I had now broken through into the selves
and pleasures of other people. So this was it.

On such red-letter days, when my unthinkably long ap-
prenticeship seemed obscene, all I could do was to scrawl
alongside my best coloratura swim the *echt,* for "genuine,"
which Ezra Pound put in the margins of Eliot's *The Waste*

Land when he thought something was all right. Then my genitals, lifting from their nest into their own peculiar tethered float, became the center around which I spun and folded and became unwound. The semi-vertigo became a bliss, the breathlessness a new rhythm to think to, and the used-up slack sensation in my shoulders and thighs the growth of innocent fresh muscle. I stretched out longer and longer, making my figure improve, tensing thongs and limbering them up in maniacal play which included a lot of maneuvering underwater with my palms differently cupped for different shapes, from egg to ball, from clay pigeon to light bulb, all wondrously malleable and shorter-lived than breaths. Or I swam with clenched fists, pretending to be an amputee, or with crossed legs that became a water plow shoved to and fro to dig my way across. I did the breaststroke using no legs at all. On cooler days, knowing the pool made twin Gulf Streams from its inlet valves on either side, I cruised the current all the way, then swam back along it with as much of me underwater as possible, hugging the wavery sausage of warmth. At season's end, while siphons drained off the surplus of the top two feet before the cover sealed up all, I went on wriggling about in the still-warm water, like a trapped life form loath to quit. I got out only to jump in again, into water that was a long way down now, below the footprints newly exposed on the vinyl liner's sides. How far the surface seemed from where it came to after heavy rains, when the pool brimmed over, pleading for someone to come dip a foot. Denied the pool, the sea, I made swimming motions on dry land or on the bed, yearning worse than an addict for the pull that draws the stomach flat and streamlines it into an aquafoil.

Each fall, after we moor the vinyl tarpaulin over the vat of joy, with water-filled plastic bags called "pigs," I vow to do next year what this year I shirked or drifted from, as un-

able to stick to a rational program of learning as to get out
of the water without jumping in again, as if, when my feet
touch the outdoor carpeting of the deck, futurity piles up
and says "You'll never swim again, you'll lose it overnight."
Back I go. It never ends. I never dream of drowning now. I
dream-swim all over the world, I who used to recall only
two dreams a year, and one of them unfailingly the one
about Jonathan Swift carrying an enormous pane of glass.
Whenever I can, I watch Burt Lancaster in *The Swimmer*,
in which he plays a man who swims home through a sub-
urb's pools to a pool he's been evicted from, or (I have lost
good taste to the chlorine water) *I Sailed to Tahiti with an
All-Girl Crew*, starring Gardner McKay and Diane McBain,
which is no more and no less than it says it is (though
hugely picturesque), and—my candidate for the worst
movie of all time—*The Mermaids of Tiburon*, but watery all
through. My mania extends to kickboards, ladders, and
long-handled skimmers; surf and shallows and shingle and
springs, and, of course, a voyeur's goodies too—beaver shots
both far and near; buoyed-up bosoms lolling on the surface
with hard-nipple bait, like apples to bob for; the uptilt of
the weightless penis like a nose with a pouch for a chin;
fronds of fern-hair flowing downstream as someone halts in
the liquid, like a stalling frog; coils of hair on the bottom,
spun by the lambent current on the top, then drifting down
intact and sodden to where surplus chlorine powder sits like
talcum in a belly button; real frogs in the skimmer basket,
fished out with a drainer spoon and set quivering back in
the brave old world of the grass. When a pool is near the
ocean, you seem to be swimming in both as the breakwater
dissolves, the windbreak blows away, and anything then
can be part of everything.

At last I learned to dive, from the steps of the shallow
end, chin down firm into the heart spoon, hands alongside

each other like upturned trowels at the end of my reach. A big smack on the top of my head was all it seemed, and then a swollen-sounding tumble of bubbles in the clanking hold of a sunken ship. I twisted into my backstroke even as I came up through the speedy fizz of it, and then dived again, amazed by the sudden end of air, the completeness of the water. Everything looked nearer than it was; a long-term memory had gone aquatic, and all those pauses the head makes when writing something down had become wedges of deep-down bubbles in no hurry to rise. I had never had so keen a sense of hiatus, and the yearning to go down, instead of up, to be the fish that lingered long with widened eyes and air enough to buddy-breathe a frog, became so strong I found myself reclining in two minds, neither of which belonged to me. I surfaced without having tried to do so, I heard the inside-out plop of diving's other end. After that, another dive, from higher up, followed by a head slam that almost made me gasp. I had a beard of suction. Even faster I went up, with the littlest body hair active in my flow, suddenly glad of the raw sunlight, where I lived.

True amphibian after all, I was a compromiser at the Plimsoll Line, happiest in two worlds at once, the one not dead, the other in no danger of being born. Would I ever snorkel? Would I ever go deep down, breathing from a tank? It didn't matter. What mattered in this mystery was mine. Just as millions of people feel less real than the so-called celebrities they fix upon, I fixed on something that made me feel as nothing. The blue water that swallows me and gives me back, as if by contract, is basically the same as the Atlantic Ocean, that uncaring slab of black, next to whose mere heedlessness the swimmer gets flash-frozen. How my dread had fueled my desire, and how my swollen self had leaped into the gulf of the never-never; and how the desire had, in a minor way, reactivated the dread, although on the level of metaphysical information, as if to tell myself to find out about the nothing while I still could know how nothing felt. So my idea of nothing ripples, heaves, and has a silken thickness: voluptuous enemy, heedless friend.

4. BREASTSTROKE TO DIVE

We can have but little pleasure and no safety in the water as indifferent swimmers. Experience proves to us that more fatal accidents happen to those who swim imperfectly than those who cannot swim at all, the latter having no temptation to expose themselves to danger.

CLIAS,
*A New and Complete Treatise
on the Art of Swimming,* 1835

A man must dream a long time in order to act with grandeur.

JEAN GENET,
Miracle of the Rose

For whom is the *Titantic* still not going down? Not as often as the sun, but several times a year, in the furry hinterland of sleep, tweaked into mind by *A Night to Remember* ('58) or a television revival, and embellished with private images of airships foundering in flames, submarines rusting on the ocean bottom (remember the *Thetis*), airplanes that come apart upside down in flight long enough for photographers to snap the obscenity, and trains that race out of control into the terminal and take it for a ride. Our highly developed sense of catastrophe never goes unexploited, but there is more to the *Titanic*—to our *Titanic* ikon—than that.

Out there, among the icebergs, with the orchestra playing and the ship becoming more and more vertical, one of the last definitive frescoes of stoicism took its cue from myth. Terror and technology came together in the presence of the stiff upper lip. A patrician concept drowned as the vision of bungling on the high seas came home to roost in the more local, less grave image of Alec Guinness, in *Kind Hearts and Coronets*, going down at the salute on the bridge of *his* ship. One can still make a sentence that brings it all together although we prefer the constituent parts of the nightmare to remain apart. *Once upon a time*, the sentence goes, *homo Icarian disregarded Mother Nature, and the rest was mere accommodation to fact.* Some people knew they were going to drown: There was just no other way, any more than there is for James Dickey's free-falling stewardess, or Auden's shot unlucky dove. Others, who knew they would not drown although they might starve or freeze, knew that hundreds would go down that night, face to face with euphemisms they'd never needed: Davy Jones's Locker, the Deep Six.

And what was inexorable included the survivors' thoughts
about the thinking of those who, aware that these were
their last thoughts for ever and ever, went on thinking
flawed, illicit, torn stuff right to the end. The mind cannot
think the mind to a halt, can it? The mind of the survivor,
in the extremest reach of compassion, cannot think the mind
of the victim to a halt either. Perhaps, even, the survivor
hates the victim-to-be because the victim can only suffer
and die. When all hope of rescue has gone, when fatheads
have attributed the rockets to a firework display and the
morse tapper had been switched off or jammed with banal
Hellos from the High Seas, immutability can sink its fangs,
and then the watchers in the boats and the doomed in the
water or still on board have a unique encounter with the
self-adjusting power of thought: to calm, to numb, to leap
toward death (as overt poems have it) like a bridegroom
into bed. That, beyond the technology and the nitty-gritty
of bungling, is what makes the *Titanic* linger in our heads:
the vision of creative fatality which brings Doctor Johnson
(who spoke of its power to concentrate a man's mind) slap-
bang before the firing squad, reprieves Saint Exupéry to
crash again in the Sahara, Admiral Byrd to be again and ter-
minally alone, and rehearses for us all the chore of last
things in the condemned mental playground.

"Hast thou ever," wrote S. T. Coleridge in one of his most
Heidegger-like moments, "raised thy mind to the consideration of EXISTENCE, in and by itself, as the mere act of
existing?" Note that he says *consideration*, which etymo-
logically speaking means to put alongside the stars. And he
exemplifies: "Hast thou ever said to thyself, thoughtfully, IT
IS! heedless in that moment, whether it were a man before
thee, or a flower, or a grain of sand?" See how he races past
the exclamation mark into "heedless" without an inter-
vening comma; such punctuation enacts his fervor. It is one
of the most suggestive, perfunctory pairs of questions in lit-

erature, not elegant but seminal, and when I too try to address myself to the is-ness of a man, a flower, a grain, I find I am trying to use my sensory apparatus to produce what each of the three is like when it has no witness. It's like trying to imagine sound waves without hearing a noise. I am using something's presence in my presence to guess at its presence in my absence, in the absence of all of us. In so doing, I do more than Heidegger when he crosses out the word *being* thus: ~~*being*~~, but leaves the deletion as a cautionary sign. I try to cross out I, but X̶ live on—an X̶ gaping at an X̶—until, one day, X̶ can gape at it no longer, X̶ am no longer allowed to gape at its spurious neatness. And then to whom, especially if it is handwritten, does it look quite the same as it did to me when X̶ was alive and full of busy blood? When others witness your deleted I while you live, you can glean something of how it will seem when you have gone, because even while you are alive nobody sees it quite as you do, and still less the "self" that underlies it, of whose flux it is the paltriest sign. Have you ever gone this way and wondered?

I   X   X̶   X̶ stet   I?

Some spoor lingers on to bewilder everyone else until there is no longer any chance to revoke bemusedly a crossed-out crossing-out with a terminal *I?*

We are absent so long, before our life and presumably after it, it might be worth thinking of our death as preexisting our life: not as the ground against which our life figures, but as the figure in which our life is grounded. When Homer, Descartes, and Swift were born, I was as good as dead; and, when millions of the unremembered were alive, I was dead also. One's death is thus vaster than one's demise, and, though one can take no credit for it, is nonetheless one's own. Vast, unique, interrupted, which a biographer might render as follows, going back to the origin of the universe: 0–1940 (say); 2010–. Those are someone's "dates." A life, that farrago of fetishes, is just one way of infiltrating and personalizing time. One's "death," before being born, is really the absence of a uniqueness-to-be, whereas one's death after one's demise consists in a uniqueness that is unrepeatable. At any rate, one's death, or absence, is something worth apprehending as part of the available context, almost as a stage set for a feat of the egotistical sublime: Before any I; during an I; then after that specific I. The problem is to jiggle the mind until what was figure becomes ground, and vice versa. The visual equivalent of this mental exercise appears more or less in the diagram below, in which a four-petaled flower or seed figures against a darker background, or a dark Maltese cross figures against a white one.

No one can see both images at the same time, and hardly anyone I've tried the drawing on "gets" the black image right away, not even when told what it is; in fact, several minutes' peering and squinting is the norm, after which, I gather, the petals or leaves somehow "empty out"—or "ungrow," "wither gray," "leak to their edges"—and flow into their background although their outlines remain, hazy and pitted. Some folk can't see the Maltese cross at all; it doesn't "click on" for them, but those who do see it exclaim in astonishment: how could it have been lurking there all the time, only a thousandth of an inch deeper, so to speak, as if embossed. Then some people feel cheated that the drawing confronts them with an either/or, as if the visual world were miserly; only the mind, abstractly taunting, can make the two images simultaneous. Visually they are never quits, any more perhaps than life and death, whereas being born and dying are more properly comparable with each other.

What happens with individual viewers is mostly the result of something white coming forward, or seeming to; it has to do with what is familiar, and I suppose four-petaled flowers are more familiar than Maltese crosses, except, say, to a German aviator of the First World War, to whom things might have been the other way round. The cross was on his plane, and so was very much in the eyes of his opponents too, just as their roundels were in his. Living thus, in this willy-nilly either/or, you have to blur your eyes in order to glimpse the best of both worlds, but you cannot go on living like that, fuzzily rich while precisely poor, reluctant to admit that our senses, our rods and cones, deprive us of such phenomena as the shaped spaces within the outline of a tree, the actual glass in a window (the texture of its transparency), the curve of a book's spine as we bend it to read. Such things are not exact equivalents of my diagram, of course, but it serves them as an emblem for the undiscerned, the un-effed, the latent, or indeed what's left after we have observed something microscopically and in the round. I mean, for instance, the etymology of a thing's name, evoking within its name's sound the successive ways in which humans tried to *utter* it, so as to make it substantially present to the mind while it was out of sight (words mimic a thing's sound or texture better than its appearance). On top of this we put the osmosis of puns: the *pucker lips* I always hear in *apocalypse,* for me an inescapable part of the word's identity. Levity? A lightness of tether, anyway, letting what's next door come in, what's linkable come near. If the unexamined life is not worthwhile, the examined life is endurable only to an open mind through which life holistically flows, keeping that mind as incomplete as our knowledge of the universe itself. Put another way, that means none of our microcosms work, and we should let them go from us, one after another, content to be a stuff which, short-leased and far from self-possessed or self-contained, can merely marvel at its tenancy.

Palping and pondering our is-ness, as Coleridge proposes, we may miss a few trains, some of what a speaker says; but the boon—not merely noises-off or gluttonous tangencies— takes us beyond our lives toward the interrogable yet gratuitous continuum that houses us: the *oikos* (Greek for *house*) which gives us the only too familiar prefix *eco-.* The very apprehensibility of things is thrilling, like a quality-beyond-qualities that only humans can relish. If, as has been argued, we have only so many ways of looking at things, so much so that peoples remote from one another in space and time duplicate one another's myths, this is one of the inevitable ways we should not skimp: this ontological awe at anything in front of us, like Everest just there. We make nothing of it, for once: no interpretation, no totem, but on a small scale we marvel at anything's being there at all as part of the many-hued, odorous, touchable, tangy, companionable medley wafting through attention's plane. The trick is that implied in a famous passage by the Venerable Peter Bede, when he likens the life of a man to "that time of which we have no knowledge." The life resembles the swift flight of a solitary sparrow through the banqueting hall where "you sit in the winter months":

This sparrow flies swiftly in through one door of the hall, and out through another. . . . Similarly, man appears on earth for a little while, but we know nothing of what went on before this life, and what follows.

Bede is grappling here with much the same figure-ground problem as I mentioned earlier, but he has not gone quite so far as to assimilate into the life the before and after, even though the flux pre-him and after-him is as unique as the one in which he is alive. We might have expected more from a Dark Ages man undertaking in one Churchillian sweep *The History of the English Church and People;* but in a way he does do it, amplifying the individual soul through congregations over the ages, thus giving the devout equivalent of what I am trying to envision in a way more pagan. He has the sense of vast void, at both ends, so to speak, but he doesn't go so far as to say "*I* was what was missing in the time of Tiberius," or "*How* would I have been if I *had* been then?" Nor does he think at all about the air the bird flies through, the smoke and soot and sparks, the air yawned and breathed, befouled and used up, air whose patterns of swirl and float, forever gone, could at one time, *at one second,* have been exactly known, given the right instruments, yet remain imaginable still as the sparrow musses them on its way from one door to another, through light from dark to dark.

Thinking about the joinedness of things, I try to capture it all in one frame, from the mites beneath a beetle's chin (it is their bus from one plant to another) to the beetle's birthplace among termites, in whose tails millions of bacteria have taken up residence and do for the termites the very thing they cannot do: digest wood, the only thing they eat.

Tree joins lawn to air, sideways as well as up and down. Lawn links low air to topsoil and what's beneath. The grass sheen on the soles of our shoes rubs chlorophyll into the tufted hemp of the doormat, the grain of the lintel-board's pine. We tread smudges of spider blood, snail track, slug ooze, ant's acid, bird and dog droppings, rain, soot, volcanic ash, bubble gum, spit, mold, oil, beetle flake, and sand into the fleece of rugs, then tread the meniscus of that thin smear back outdoors. We make a Man Friday palimpsest. Daily we tread fainter and fainter overlays "into being": both ways, which means we *create* them anew each day, and we tromp them into—in among—what's already there. We puff at the trees which, like the Atlantic City of old, do enough rebreathing to be called the Lungs of Philadelphia. Heedlessly, tinily, we remix the physics of being by just moving around. We are a part of all that we have never been. Born of the sun, we leave footprints on the moon.

Each time we stir, air makes and remakes exact molds of us with never a trace to the eye; yet we make millions of these transient displacements, which do not exist unless we are within them, but could only be seen when we were not. Lined up in translucent series over us, what would they be like? See-through robot suits or a combination of diaphanous spoons and tureens, comfortable cling-film mannikins one behind the other: the sum total of our apparitions in rough Indian file, vastly alike but different enough not to fit into one another. The lower air teems with our phantoms yet endlessly opens to receive us. Only in water do you feel the backwash, the undertow, of where you only just now were; you leave a more enduring spoor, you meet your recent self more often, aspin in the suction of a cavity your wallow has filled, your bubbles have signed.

A blue-green fighter jet has just shot over, only a hundred feet up, at something short of sonic speed, and the conical whoosh of its going was the side-spill of all the air pile-

print washed away, and, for him, the premonition of a
stmortem world in which that fact is paramount.

This extreme view of the self and of objects is what we
et instead of a view that's infinite. Instead of touching a
ower with mind and hand, touch it with everything else as
well: nose, chin, cheek, Adam's apple, knee, ankle, toetip,
armpit hair, the space between two toes, and, if possible
working up to nipple, penis, vulva, or whatever else. You
never forget this supplement to your sensuous record of that
particular flower. (Going back to Coleridge, it is easier to
deal with a flower in this way than with a human being or a
grain of sand: the former might get you arrested, the latter
so contorted that you may never straighten up again.) All it
amounts to, really, is filching a leaf or two from the book of
the handicapped, who, with spontaneous disregard for decorum, help themselves to a sensuous gamut we others are
denied—or deny ourselves. So too with words: millions of
dead speakers and musers are behind me, diffidently choric
in my mind's ear, when I utter the word *flower*, say.* Words
of the most commonplace kind are memorial root systems
from the gone, who come into play in manifold simplicity
whenever we ask for an ice cream cone. The dead are never
dead so long as we are using language, although even a society of gestures alone might guarantee them immortality.
The continuity is the lease we have on life. And future
speakers, or gesturers, will bring *us* back into play too, even
if they talk in mathematical symbols and gesture only with
prosthetic limbs a mile away. The extreme view of death I
have already tried to explain: It amounts to pondering and
probing your two absences while you are present enough to
do it—what you would have said to Sappho if you'd known
her, or what a future interlocutor won't be able to say to
you because you won't be around to be addressed. If that

* Ninety-one percent of all the people who have ever lived, says Arthur H.
Westing of Amherst College.

driven up in front of it, getting out of
gross blob of gas in which we spin, which
lessly, cupping, yielding, cushioning, chan
ing, a jug of plenty brewed by greenwoo
nous is next to numinous. Air has no memor
least, any more than a deity needs a potato pe
somehow blatant, but air is the caviar of eleme
to water's Sousa; requiring finer attunements. I h
water before I could graduate to air, on whose
doted long before I had the faintest notion of w
were cleaving through: not just the whipped cre
cumulo-cirrus, but what the ancients called *aether*, p
sor of the ether which anesthetists let hiss when
wanted to put you out. Yet air is not, as we say, ethereal
all, sibling of mist and fog, dew and steam. Invisible host
the Rayleigh scattering which blues both sky and sea, it i
the Maltese cross in my now-you-see-it/now-you-don't emblem: the layer that leads to zero and sometimes looks exactly like it. And when more things than usual come together, I try to link air to death, trying to assimilate all the
shapes that have passed through it with the invisibility of
the dead, trying, trying, to see air and death as figures
against the ground of us. Not cozy. We evolve, they do not.
We are the process, they the constants. Once they have had
us, they do not have us again, and we have not so much
vanished as deprived them of us. So I try to think, half
vengefully, half superior, of what the sum of things lacked
before I was, and what it will lose when I go. Time with two
gaps in it: the achieved self shoved into the gap before
birth, and as a known quantity interrupting the everyday
hereafter. Kilroy into baby Kilroy's blank; Kilroy into
Kilroy's life; and then this second envisioning a third, which
is Kilroy in the act of anticipating the unique absence the
world will one day force him to impose on it. Man Friday's

driven up in front of it, getting out of its way. I salute the gross blob of gas in which we spin, which rolls with us, endlessly, cupping, yielding, cushioning, changing, and renewing, a jug of plenty brewed by greenwood trees. Voluminous is next to numinous. Air has no memory, not of *us*, at least, any more than a deity needs a potato peeler. Water is somehow blatant, but air is the caviar of elements, a Delius to water's Sousa; requiring finer attunements. I had to learn water before I could graduate to air, on whose vehicles I doted long before I had the faintest notion of what they were cleaving through: not just the whipped cream of cumulo-cirrus, but what the ancients called *aether*, precursor of the ether which anesthetists let hiss when they wanted to put you out. Yet air is not, as we say, ethereal at all, sibling of mist and fog, dew and steam. Invisible host to the Rayleigh scattering which blues both sky and sea, it is the Maltese cross in my now-you-see-it/now-you-don't emblem: the layer that leads to zero and sometimes looks exactly like it. And when more things than usual come together, I try to link air to death, trying to assimilate all the shapes that have passed through it with the invisibility of the dead, trying, trying, to see air and death as figures against the ground of us. Not cozy. We evolve, they do not. We are the process, they the constants. Once they have had us, they do not have us again, and we have not so much vanished as deprived them of us. So I try to think, half vengefully, half superior, of what the sum of things lacked before I was, and what it will lose when I go. Time with two gaps in it: the achieved self shoved into the gap before birth, and as a known quantity interrupting the everyday hereafter. Kilroy into baby Kilroy's blank; Kilroy into Kilroy's life; and then this second envisioning a third, which is Kilroy in the act of anticipating the unique absence the world will one day force him to impose on it. Man Friday's footprint washed away, and, for him, the premonition of a postmortem world in which that fact is paramount.

This extreme view of the self and of objects is what we get instead of a view that's infinite. Instead of touching a flower with mind and hand, touch it with everything else as well: nose, chin, cheek, Adam's apple, knee, ankle, toetip, armpit hair, the space between two toes, and, if possible working up to nipple, penis, vulva, or whatever else. You never forget this supplement to your sensuous record of that particular flower. (Going back to Coleridge, it is easier to deal with a flower in this way than with a human being or a grain of sand: the former might get you arrested, the latter so contorted that you may never straighten up again.) All it amounts to, really, is filching a leaf or two from the book of the handicapped, who, with spontaneous disregard for decorum, help themselves to a sensuous gamut we others are denied—or deny ourselves. So too with words: millions of dead speakers and musers are behind me, diffidently choric in my mind's ear, when I utter the word *flower*, say.* Words of the most commonplace kind are memorial root systems from the gone, who come into play in manifold simplicity whenever we ask for an ice cream cone. The dead are never dead so long as we are using language, although even a society of gestures alone might guarantee them immortality. The continuity is the lease we have on life. And future speakers, or gesturers, will bring *us* back into play too, even if they talk in mathematical symbols and gesture only with prosthetic limbs a mile away. The extreme view of death I have already tried to explain: It amounts to pondering and probing your two absences while you are present enough to do it—what you would have said to Sappho if you'd known her, or what a future interlocutor won't be able to say to you because you won't be around to be addressed. If that

---

* Ninety-one percent of all the people who have ever lived, says Arthur H. Westing of Amherst College.

smacks too much of the dizzy blur when trying to see the white flower in the same instant as the black Maltese cross, blame evolution. We can see either plainly or choose to let a double image shimmer at us as we rise and fall in the shallow well of the double emblem like a jump jet that can't make up its mind. Living mortals are entitled to ambivalence, driven from trying to say what they mean to, in the end, hoping to mean what they end up saying.

I have just looked again at both white flower and Maltese cross, still trying to snatch the two in one glimpse; but it never works although it nearly works, and the petals flash forward frayed, the cross recedes as if newly peeled. Some would call it phenomenology, which lets you entertain whatever sense data come your way, but it might be *duopan* as well: a double All. The term matters less than the somewhat unnerving unavailability of the twin images during what we like to think is the same visual act. Yet it is reassuring too. We tend to think of death in terms of life, rarely of death in death terms only, which is misleading, as is thinking about our lives only in terms of death, which is common. In the diagram, although you can mentally associate white with black as freely as you want, they remain discrete: alternative neighbors who do not speak. What an odd thing, to be thus impeded in a physical universe that allows elementary particles to be shot at one another, to collide, yet to produce pieces no smaller than the original particles. The high energy of the impact has turned into matter. This so amazed and delighted Werner Heisenberg that, in his *Across the Frontiers,* he mentioned it twice, adding "we have thus arrived at the boundary where the concept of division loses its meaning."

By this token, not only division loses its meaning, but also the tremendous arsenal of old-fashioned and new-fangled philosophical systems; indeed, the hunt for meaning—on which the whole western educational system, together with its religious-philosophical encampments, bases itself—goes down the chute. Whereas we used to look for explanations, and even tried to justify the ways of God to Man, nowadays we have trouble enough in creating an accurate description of what nature is like, which means that the job of literature is not to fudge up bogus cosmologies but to describe what is there and to express its woof, its texture, in full. Intimidating and awe-inspiring as subatomic particles are, they do not foster superstition so much as a renewed sense of how elaborately arbitrary, how gratuitous, the core of nature is. A fluke generating trillions of other flukes, amid which, to recall Heisenberg, the lost concept of division almost blurs life into death, and vice versa. We never belong to ourselves, or to one another. We thrive in the mindless play of particles to which, in the long run, even our own star will return. "Knee-deep in the cosmic overwhelm," as one of my tutor's loveliest lines expresses it, we are small grains in a colossal, heedless harvest, and our main chore, beyond the describing of it all, is to say how we feel about it, in hymns of blissful terminal indignation without, however, having any entity to blame, so long as we are thinking about death from natural causes and not Nazi bombers, or terrorists, muggers, and industrial smog.

In a sense, to write such a sentence is to say good-bye; I have no hope of ever getting beyond it, unless I decide to fool myself after all and chuck in my lot with this or that pack of obscurantists. That is why I find the old engrossing, not the young; the old, in their nearness to being cut down, and with no hope (as with those elementary particles) of ending up more numerous and enlarged, are more terrifying than the young, in their ungrateful indifference to being alive. Both groups belong to the universe, but the old have begun to discover in full the waning differentiation the young don't know about; the old mind hears the tocktick of cells failing and knows the daily erosion of an almost Faustian debt that has to be repaid. Yet the mind, knowing, can do nothing to halt the process, and this gradual going back into nature, this high dream being tripped by an inexorable low foot, invites a devastating humility that is only an option, of course. You can go down raving, damning every instant of it, even invoking the name of the scientist—Leonard Hayflick—who identified the cutoff point in human cells, when they begin to make mistakes and cease to heal. It makes no difference, even if mind over matter includes our power over elementary particles through sheer intensity of thought. The bad old cells will get you in the end through a mere quirk in matter. The old are the universe at its most conscious, trapped near the terminus with a bit of mind extant but much of the body already lost, and trying to satisfy a racial need to come to some conclusion—an ultimate sense-making—before coming to that other one. Holy dying, as Jeremy Taylor has it, must be unresentful stuff, as full of gorgeous and sonorous piety as Taylor's prose, whereas what I feel is more like enraptured aversion, in which, through some urge to test things to the maximum, I obsessively finger the different strands of being—petals, hands, bark of trees, the hunch of the aged—and end up deploring the automatic quality of so much compared to the nimble undulations of the mind (and never mind how predictable they seem to some).

That is how I interpret my teenage brush with pneumonia, whose slime, because it almost took me off in the days before antibiotics, twins with water in my chamber of wet horrors and sends me to the novelty of so-called "mucodynes," which cut and dilute the mucus until it arrives at the indivisible minimum envisioned by bunged-up philosophers. Its very name means snot exploded. A clear amberlike syrup breaks the disulphide bonds that crosslink proteins in our phlegm and alters local ionic charges that keep the polysaccharides together. All this in order to cough it up. It's as if two chain-link fences have been wrecked, one of ordinary wire, the other electrified. And then we are well. Nature "husbands" itself so neatly, even in the spaces between molecules of mucus; and yet, while dishing up such deathly forms of life in death, also lets there be mucodynes, which snap the nasty links in what we can't cough up and run their battery dead. If this sketch of Mother Nature, red in tooth and claw but also rudely just, offends, it's only because it's paradoxical; but so was evolution, succeeding through trial and error, squirming around until it hit on a worthwhile program, a way of getting to tomorrow. *Diplococcus pneumoniae* had an even chance.

As I think Coleridge sensed, to contemplate the is-ness of things is exhausting; it's as if you are powering the thing itself with mental jumper cables; but nothing vivifies even that experience more than the thought that this is what death precludes, and then you contemplate is-ness with near-fanatical zeal, making it majestic, dense, and beyond words. So too with the *Titanic*, that big-scale Raft of the Medusa littered with so many last things—last thoughts, last smiles, last words—that the mind aches to engage it; yet engage it we do, like insomniacs probing tongue into the tooth that burns.

"Eschatology" is the mouthwash word we use: last things accomplished by the actual doomed, and last things guessed at—ours, theirs, anyone's—in a trance of inverted empathy. Surely the mind switches off? Or it so transmutes the immediate hurt that it becomes as an after-dinner's sleep. Or, and here we shudder like De Quincey frightening himself half to death by staring at Lord Rosse's ghoulish drawing of the Great Nebula in Orion, does the mind rise to undreamed-of excesses in self-torture? Does the mind mind? It knows it minds, and what it does, perhaps, in ultimate self-defense, is to suppress the factor of fatality, rising to such control of itself as to blot death out. As Eliot says, some conditions look remarkably like one another, can flourish in the same hedgerow, and perhaps the mind, creator of categories, has final power over them, to abolish and efface. It should; otherwise, from a pragmatic point of view, it's just no good to us. The *Titanic* was full of people who'd never worried about that sort of thing, or who'd had experts do their worrying for them. Then, out of the blue, they were up against it, the ontology of the penultimate, and there was no time to think it out. What we remember, maybe in the penumbra of Scott of the Antarctic's friend, Captain Oates, going out into the snow to die, is the composure of all those people, many of them enacting without knowing the Latin the words of Seneca: *fatis agimur, cedite fatis.* The fates have us, so give in. And then, the myth would like to say, they all live more richly in their last hour than in all their years before. With discipline it might be done. Some no doubt did it, but what of those who didn't? What did they say to themselves?

There must be at least two stages in this little marathon of will. The approach may be quite unrealistic, even after being dumped in the water and becoming involved in the suction down. But the ensuing moments, after the held breath fizzles out, evoke the victim in the gas chamber, who's told to fill both lungs and get it over with (whereas the person electrocuted is wholly passive). What happens, I wonder, when you willy-nilly inhale water and become part of the ocean? If you hold your breath until you pass out, then you inhale water unknowingly. Otherwise, you do it with repugnance or, just perhaps, with Shelleyan relish, as a last act of defiantly collaborative drowning akin to inhaling warm saltwater to clear the sinuses. The nostrils sting. The sink beneath the pharynx feels flooded. You swallow, but this time there is far too much to swallow and the water makes its leaden way into the lung. You inhale more than you breathe out. There is no air to vent it into, and all you are is a rebellious valve, dressing the water in a new suit of pulmonary tissue, the only sense of danger being that distant, heavyweight heartburn, surely someone else's, it feels so general, so vague.

That, presumably, is the good way, not fighting at all, inviting Nature in to complete an inevitable tryst. But, as Camus said, in his 1951 "Homage to André Gide," "To die is such appalling torture for some men that it seems to me as if a happy death redeems a small patch of creation." Surely the converse is true too. The torture of reluctant drowning befouls the Creation that doesn't treat us all alike, and some people have no control over how the last cupful, that might have made their tea, crumbled a bouillon cube, or soaked a misplaced stamp from its corner of an envelope, enters the lung, making it bulge still bigger.

What does that two-hundred-yard-long gash in the ship's hull, slit by the iceberg's knife below the waterline, tell us about our ordinary lives on land? What, never mind how tacitly, does it bring into play, almost after the manner of abstract expressionism, nibbling at us from just outside the range of vision without ever obtruding? Does that dreadful marine fresco make all other things seem trivial, as if death or disaster on land were a trifle compared to death by water, water in the midst and the bowels of breath, the final glutted choke severing even the final trope of grace under pressure? Even our belated response to the *Titanic* has a provisional, expendable quality: slanted for loss, as if we've just remembered Beckett, who reminds us to turn away just in time from things about to disappear, such as the *Titanic* drowner going down for the last time. Think of that drowner, if you can. He implies perishability; our tininess on the land of our planet, flailing in its seas, even walking the promenade deck of an ocean liner. Not that he deals up the overlapping twins, micro- and macrocosm (the frail bark of the self aboard the argosy that floats upon a globe floating in Archimedean space); he cannily eschews routine obeisances and instead fixes on things and their vanishing points, setting up loose structures from which they can easily fall away, or through which they can drop. The I has no tenure, any more than the sea knows what it is. (I write this in Pittsburgh, at a window opposite the U. S. Steel skyscraper, blocked off from me this minute by a solid snow squall that makes the building look less durable than snow; the squall will pass, but snow will outlive U. S. Steel.) This intuition of several brevities we put into the sealed mouth of the *Titanic* drowner, who is about to go under not because he or she is unable to think of anything new, but because essentially there hasn't been anything new for a long time.

The point comes from Galileo who, accepting the nothing new (evolution lets us last only so long), declares our own demise useful: We make room for other life. How this cheerless clear-eyed un-"narrow" point of view bears on lives prematurely but lingeringly closed, only the individual can decide, opting perhaps for one of the following: 1. The deaths from the *Titanic* disaster diminished all of mankind, leaving an irremediable gash in the race. 2. It didn't matter. There are always people to replace people with. 3. Captains shouldn't be reckless, oblivious, or fatheads. 4. All such disasters instruct us in the human condition, which is lethal and full of bad luck; the longer you last (in one sense), the more bad luck you get. Would we lament the *Titanic* less if it had been full of nonagenarians all with terminal illness? I think not. We'd argue that even they, with "full lives" behind them, had paid their passage money and were entitled to a trouble-free cruise. In the end, it's a matter of incongruity. You die, not because there are icebergs, but because some idiot drives his ship too fast. And then the long, pensive, utterly terminal wait until you go into the frigid water. The snag isn't, overtly, the famous absurdity of things, but the irrational quality of human behavior, at one extreme the hotrod skipper, at another utmost composure in the very teeth of death; and perhaps the core of our disheveled horror is this: If we were wholly rational beings, we'd find life more intolerable than we do; but, since we often behave as weirdly as the universe itself does, we can counter its weirdness with our own, and what Henry James called the insolence of accident unhinges us less. Maybe the wholly rational person *in extremis* can create a flawless composure, simply accepting the ways of God to Man, but it's more likely that more of us are helped by the palliative of what's irrational—not *I can't do anything about it, so I won't think about it* but *Let me come up with something that will keep me from seeing it for what it is*. Not truth but blarney. Not fact but ritual. Not so but otherwise. Ship of fools? Hardly. Every fool makes a serious final act. No fool is denied it. And no fool is as foolish as these figures, cited like the numbers of hymns:

	Women and Children Saved	Men Saved	Total Saved
First Class	94%	31%	60%
Second Class	81%	10%	44%
Steerage	47%	14%	25%
Crew	87%	22%	24%

Such were the first statistics; then bodies began to appear as much as forty-five miles from the ship's last radioed position. The *Bremen* saw almost a hundred and fifty, including a man in evening dress still afloat on a door, other bodies in steamer chairs, a couple of men arm in arm, and one woman floating like Ophelia with her nightgown bellied out in the surface wind. Scandinavian immigrants journeying to Minnesota reported seeing their boat hit bodies and knock them out of the water several feet into the air. The number of survivors changed slightly, but the percentages remained the same. Over 1,500 had been lost—1,513 or 1,517 (the final count varies even now†)—and perhaps even that miserable diaspora of corpses, scattered ever wider with the motion of the Gulf Stream and the break-up of the ice, is a more human, more assimilable image of last things than that given by percentages divided by sex, age, and social class. Anonymous horror has no bite, even if you talk in millions, which are too easily said. Convenient as they may be for computers, their jockeys, and their grooms, mere numbers are another form of blank. People and stars need names, as do telephone exchanges too.

For the full apprehension of such baleful arithmetic, you need the news wire from April 15, 1912: "All passengers of the *Titanic* have boarded the lifeboats safely and in calm waters." There was no one else, between life and death, for anyone to be; no halfway house on that darkling plain of slop; no half-measure when it came to drowning or being saved. With the disaster distanced by empty time, the iceberg can roam about in anyone's *Titanic*-haunted head, like something cooked up by Artaud: an incomprehensible, enigmatic object corresponding to nothing at all and creating

† Another version is H. M. Enzensberger's in *The Sinking of the Titanic;* for reasons unknown, his totals include Steerage and Crew only:

	First	Second	Steerage		Crew		Total
Embarked	325	285	1,316	+	885	=	2,201
Saved	203	118	499	+	212	=	711
Lost	122	167	817	+	673	=	1,490

Correctly added, his sub-totals of the Lost make 1,779, creating a phantom contingent of some 289 souls; no number is blanker than that. Perhaps he is making a covert political point—only the poor and the crew were real.

nothing less than awe. Featureless, it monolithically counterpoints the host of saliences that compose the ship, much
as the sound of it—a high-pitched zipper slowing as it closes
—counterpoints the soothing twaddle bleated by the band—
a medley from *The Dollar Princess*. If there is something
eerie about a stratified mini-society floating across three
thousand miles of blank, uncaring ocean, with every quirk
and comfort transplanted, there is something even eerier
when that society gets its death sentence and, with only
hours to live, works itself into the paroxysms or the super-
charged protocols of the end of a world. It's like *fin de siècle*
all squashed up into the span of a three-hour examination,
and that pressure—the pressure upon any poet to distill and
foreshorten—works its way into our black-rot dreams.

The moral point that emerges is not only the semi-
triumphant one, vague as it is, of being obligated to swim
and never to give in to death until it seizes us (postlude to
Camus's notion of refusal), but also that, even to set about
depicting and reenacting such a catastrophe (or an atrocity,
say) involves you as an accomplice. You become the perpe-
trator, even if only a bit; and, where the catastrophe is "natural," the hitherto absent culprit, a stand-in for the faceless
chthonic force. This role upsets anyone who cannot separate
the picking and choosing that goes into everyday living
from, here at any rate, the role of a Fate repeating a notori-
ous past performance.

Who would not, then, almost dote on the passengers, who
enliven such lethal work? Not in their categories—the
steerage drunks, the toffs in their tuxedos, the five Chinese
stowaways—but as flotsam agonists, individuals forced to
an unthinkable extreme, given a time limit, yet surrounded
more or less with the paraphernalia of social class, of ship-
board leisure, and still, in spite of themselves, thinking it
cannot possibly happen, not to them. Even amid the prelim-
inary panic there is time for usual observances: cigar ash

volunteered for death by drowning. Of course, there is the doom of death, about which it seems the dead are not free to meditate, but there is also the doom of the survivors who have been spared for a different death. They have looked the ineluctable in the eyes and come home. I spent a year trying to learn that feeling from what the survivors of the 1944 bomb plot against Hitler finally made known; mostly they seemed to have earned the right to climb down from the pinnacle of matters epic and to spend the rest of their days in somnambulistic mundanity, listening to their bodies creak and gurgle: to their vital signs. In one sense these men and women, after 1944, were irrevocably linked with Hitler's survival in 1944 and his death in 1945, drenched in *his* history rather than in their own; and the *Titanic* survivors, as their history implies, were irrevocably linked with the sea, a force upon whose side we find ourselves, mortifiedly thrilled, daunted by the winner. With what intricate relish we evoke its horrors, their gradualness, their indivisibility from paddling pools, goldfish bowls, drains and dew, without ever rising to the level of sentient metaphor that enables Proust, in his impromptu-feeling essay on Flaubert's style, to join our lack of embarrassment for having slept to the altogether more putative lack of embarrassment (or confusion) "when we come to realize, someday, that we have made the momentary passage of death." If you set Hans Magnus Enzensberger's book-length Titanic poem alongside, say, the "Grief and Oblivion" section of *Albertine disparue*, something emerges about the psychological healing power of exact metaphors, or, if not healing power, then power to widen the sense of human experience so much that, because life seems fuller and keener, death is somehow cheated. I think that is what Shelley meant when he spoke of poets as "the hierophants of an unapprehended inspiration; the mirrors of the gigantic shadows which futurity casts upon the present; the words which express what

into the ashtray, of course, opening doors for ladies,
"after you, sir." One wonders just how far etiquette can
just a human to an act of God, or indeed if there isn't a
tocol of staring death down. Yes, the British dressed for c
ner in the bowels of the jungle, but the people on
Titanic had a chance to push correct behavior all the way
the end of the line. Could it denature death, converting i
sting into a *faux pas?* Could drowning (or freezing) b
downgraded, through a final series of exquisitely wille
amenities, into something like a vulgarism? Or a dull day, a
walk in the wet, a Lent of the mind? The individuals are
there on the ship, but we see only their iceberg tips, and it
is like revisiting some of Eliot's crisper portrait collections,
those little communities of one-line snubs ("Hakagawa,
bowing among the Titians").

The poignant saliences are there of course: from the
First-Class dinner menu to the first radiogram "*0015 hours
CQ Position 41° 46′ North 50 14′ West*," and these take their
place in our minds all over again as our society, with deliberately averted eye, *reminds* us by *A Night to Remember*,
not that bad a movie, and *Titanic* ashtrays, *Titanic* T-shirts,
as if we come to this theme backhandedly, through its shod-
diest appearances in popular lore, which puts us in the position of searching for the *Real Titanic*, hardly available at
all, and raises the question I raised at the beginning: How
can we know except through empathy? It is typical of us
that we should feel easiest with the *Titanic*'s myth, where it
is most an emblem, and least easy with how the victims'
consciousnesses died.

Eventually the seagulls that have followed the *Titanic*
across the ocean, and have hovered about it while it goes
down, wheel away to find another ship: soothsaying, doom-
saying gulls, those, with nothing more to say to those more
than 1,500 seafarers who, although having put themselves
briefly outside the timetables of the land, have certainly not

they understand not," and when he credited metaphor with "the before unapprehended relations of things." Two "unapprehended"s is par for him, of course.

Whether they are right or wrong, it's our visions—our emblems of extruded hope—that say the most about our individuality or uniqueness, whether, in regretting the *Titanic*, we go down with it, open as an exposed ribcage, or, still bobbing brightly and expertly about in safe water this side of the reef, we just quip that the name of the deathship sank an adjective as well. Whenever I swim, I think about the *Titanic*, long before my time as it was, not because I called one of my tight-lipped water scowls after it, but because those people drowned, *en masse*, in a savage hyperbole of the fate I myself had dreaded, and into which I go on prying even now that I have become semi-competent. Drowning with discipline and dignity, I still suppose, is much like learning to swim. Or you do both with panic, and the result is still the same. That foundered Titan is my ikon. I am among the helpless still.

Yet, when the water mood has me, I blur my eyes and my lashes turn into frail stalactites or stalagmites against the pearly blur of day: I am swimming where I sit, but in much vaster motion, in a whirling room within an orbit around a star that goes where its galaxy goes, the Galaxy whose center is a scab of solid-looking silver. Dizzy, I hear the hum of its radiance, I smell the gaudy blues and greens of its gases, I tremble with its blind eye upon me, and in a slight shift sideways—the width of a thimble or the thickness of my trunks—I have traveled a billion miles in a big breaststroking swoosh. I don't come back. Hundreds call my name, but I have gone into the galaxy where my father is tweaking his nose and wishing he had more privacy. And what this means is that I sky-ify the water, since air is much more like a nothing than water is, which feels too solid to be the noth-

ingness it is. Yet, truly, I should be testing water against a
vacuum like the stratosphere, whose wafer-thin inhospital-
ity is as tough on air breathers as pools and seas. I dwin-
dle or grow fat in what I call dimensions; when in air, I am
in all the air; when in sky, am in all the sky; when in water,
am in all the water in the world, which reaches before and
after me like an elemental canoe whose tips are out of sight.
If a bit is all, then shouldn't *all* amount to only a smidgeon?
I think it does. I minify, reducing all that's made to a
breath, a two-inch telescope, and an inkwell. I am each
cough, each matt-gray disk of sky, each dip of the pen. And
at my most honest I cough up that leaden penny of sky and
gob it into the inkwell, I drink the ink and tint the heavens
with it, I swallow the lensful of sky and dip my pen into my
mouth even while coughing up ink. The partitions break
down. They were never there, not in my mind; and when I
swim or float, I think a liquid gibberish in which *I salmon*
becomes a verb form, water can dangle, sky can splash, and
there are stars in trunks diving off phosphorescent diving
boards into vats of petunias. I go afield, gathering hydrogen, and throw sheaves of it from the pool onto the lawn.
Have I imagined it, or did the Milky Way shimmer in the
pool one moonless night like a worn-out feather boa? Slithering in, I swam up its length, at least from Orion to Sagit-
tarius, blowing bubbles at each constellation as I passed it
(if I remembered them aright). After that, on the return, I
thought I was curled around a limb of a new blue star, tight
as a leech around an orange, only to be thrown off and away
in a stellar prominence that took me right back to the glint-
ing ladder and the damp mat beyond it, where the toes re-
tightened for the walk along the deck while, overhead, the
assembled star stuff droned and honked, buzzed and
brimmed. I always feel as if elsewhere. The pool's deck is
the *Titanic's*.

Leaving the pool, and feeling even heavier-footed on the

felt-lined planks of the deck than I was in the water, I seem to slip, not so much on the puddles my feet make on a polished floor indoors as into space, sideways, with my water-logged trunks heavy and squeaking: the ballast for an off-balance shunt into air which feels as if it has just been full of water. I lurch, I topple, I slither up again. I seem to be no longer myself, perhaps as an eye minus a retina is no longer an eye.

Again I do one of my water tricks, staring at the sun like Isaac Newton until I can bear the blaze no longer and I shut my eyes tight on a retina image of seething purple that begins to turn brown. Then, from tiptoe or ungainly tread, I flop forward into a surface dive and open my eyes underwater to watch the sun cool down. But it is never there, washed or faded away along with the tiny tadpole- or sperm-shapes that flit across my sight whenever I aim closed lids at the sun. I am the pearl diver who first captures his solar trophy, then plunges to lose it, a spendthrift of daily light, always coming up for more to squander. You can do this with the moon too, most of all when it is full, but you have to stare at it through a telescope for quite a while, at least until your eyes begin to ache, and then race into the water before the image on the retinas wanes. Too much trouble, too little blaze, whereas playing Newton with the sun is like being branded deep inside the head. No hiss as the ingot goes away, but the sense of having gone below with a piece of the sun, permanganate lapsing into khaki, *that* is sublime enough to last, yet never too good to be done all over again. It's a way of playing tag with just one star. I get out only to reel back into the water. I reel into it only to get out again the better to savor the next immersion. Out, I have a keener sense of in; and in, I pull the whole world after me, in doused possessive joy.

Everything streams into me and through me; I am a crystal lattice, a dunce's cap of grease-proof paper, and the whole gamut of my swim—birdsong, termite wings, the blue carbolic stench of chlorine, globes of blue water rolling along my abdomen, tidal pulls between my toes, the dwindling chill of first immersion—dominate whatever it is I'm trying to think until, although in air, I am back in the water again, this time in a shiny mental bubble of it. Seen through, I see through, much as during a migraine attack you can see both your outstretched hand and what's behind it; the migraine sufferer, who sees dazzling saw teeth and shimmering battlements and soaring white spots like studs of chromium come loose, is in fact looking at the process of sight itself. His eye system has come so far unstuck that, in going wrong, it permits a view into the bowels of its error. So too with the after-swim: I swim within the swimming process once I leave the water, I walk as if floating, I do fall, and sometimes am quick enough to convert the fall that comes from being suddenly out of that other element into the fall that's just the skid of a slippery foot. No one is watching, but I am still inhibited enough to mind feeling off-balance while walking web-footed down a polished hallway, pursing my lips for the upbrimming line of the water.

Ecstasy I have to call it: when I am thrown or hurled clean out of my usual being, out of my customary doldrum into first, yes, the swamping vault of the mesmeric blue water, but then into this other thing, when my nose seems to see and my eyes let the water dip into my soul, and then comes the exaltation after the exultation, the spell after the thrill—ecstasy's thumbprint skeined silver. My flesh feels like a lot of confetti stuck together, conjecturally light and likely to crumble in a bit of wind. Breathing has become so shallow it doesn't move the chest, but all the breath is in the bottom of my throat, flanking the windpipe and going nowhere. My feet are jelly, my hands are light as bamboo and perforated like the backs of chairs. The tips of my teeth are rough with non-existent sand. My hair has been thumped into my scalp and my genitals have withered into a baby fig. I find it hard to sift the actual physical sensation of the moment from what seems to be outright hallucination; it's as if I come into the house on a wave, wafted, a ghost of myself. Swum out: That's the condition, of course, but the mind has become too busy for any version that prosaic, and, right there in the big bowl of the mind's eye, the moon comes out of hiding, the sun looms and begins to wobble, the clouds lather themselves ready to shave, and a waterspout of blue water pours into the sky. Not bad, this mix or pan-mixis, until other beings, and their cries, begin moving through me, while my stomach growls like a distant dog, a Peke maybe. *Right, scrub everything!* comes one voice, blotted out by the one that yells *Get it at Redgates* (no mystery to me; Redgates was my favorite toyshop in the city where I went on the bus as a child). Then the obsessive words begin, much more frightening; one day it's *Surabaya,* the next it's *griffon.* Someone playing with a thermostat—cooling and heating, then combining auto fan with either—is in much the same position, but in my case the thermostat is adjusting itself.

For several hours the hallucinogen of swim makes everyday things almost too sharp to be endured. Brass screws flock out of a see-through plastic cylinder like roaches. In the faces of total strangers, I infallibly detect a slight grimace from their most recent orgasm. Someone forking a Swiss steak in Friendly's seems tethered to the meat and trying to pull free. And commonplace words in ordinary combinations (Where's the instant coffee?) don't seem to express what they should, are either null and blank or hopelessly baroque, and I wonder what to say instead, hoping by indirection to find direction out. I always used to say, when teased about my compulsions (having the bedclothes exactly smooth and straight and newspapers folded up after reading as if new), *my head is full of pandemonium, I want*

things on the outside to be tidy! There was a time when, out
of mingled insecurity and abstractedness, I kept buying
extra loaves of white Italian bread, uneasy to be without,
and then, similarly inspired, the same with packets of instant mashed potato (in this instance going so far as always
to have a packet of it in my briefcase or my flight bag,
aghast at the prospect of being trapped somewhere without
a pabulum soft enough; that water might be lacking, with
which to mix my paste, never occurred to me). Post-swim,
though, is a pandemonium worse than the old mental chaos
ever was, and I have learned to live within it, actually
reveling in it even when it is spiky and senseless, when it
sets me pitching sideways with a bad smell in my head and
nothing to hold on to, and I soothe myself in pinball arcades
with machines that test my grip, all the way from "See a
Doctor" to "Superman," although I rarely budge the finger
of muscular fate beyond "Women: Good, Men: Average,"
and as often as not can't get it past "Sissy."

New-born, I was constipated for a week, and my parents
were ready to cart me off to the hospital when, at first long
last, I *moved*, with, as my mother says, "a bang." Maybe,
having been always constipated as a child, I carried around
with me the ghost of that extra freight, and so threw my
center of gravity off, or rather threw off my notion of where
it was, thinking I was heavier than I was. And so on. Some
mental holdup, throwback, stowaway, kept me from my
water paradise. Not only was I nervous, I was nervously
heavy or heavy-minded, and not only that: I was both nervously and heavy-mindedly compulsive, as well as traumat-
ically addicted to liquids, mashed potatoes and mashed
peas, the softness of pillow and of bread. No wonder I went
nowhere in the water, and these things link up with my
much more recent passion, in matters verbal, never to create
a style more boring than the vacancy that was there before
it. For all that time, decade after decade, I was somewhat in

the fix of the stroke victim (what a gentle word "stroke," for *that*) who blinks spasmodically but cannot even cry, so receiving artificial tears that sting. Be brave, I told myself. You can't have everything—God is the author of the system that has wiped out every creature so far born since the origin of life. Who are you to whine? Yet when swimming came, and then the psychic vertigo of after-swimming's ecstasy, I didn't fare too badly, getting more than I'd bargained for: tickled pink, yet always wondering if all this fun would wipe the real thing out, and I'd been given yet another substitute, another second best; a year of swimming at the most and then, final as death, never again to float, to splash, to tread; not even to wade with the old kid's confidence.

Sometimes, almost underwater, I feel as if I am swimming through the atmosphere toward the Red Spot in Jupiter, with a telescope strapped to my head, and beginning to see where I am going in this dark, as space curves to receive and make a chair to cup my back. It's perfect then. Or when I deliberately break a float, and, in between the almost symphonic memory of that dead-limb halt and the first tiny shear of the beginning stall or sideslip, there comes a pinpoint of languor stretched past breaking but not yet broken, and I am the surplus ripple that begins the sough that, ever so reluctantly, will take me down, or at least askew. At those watersheds I thrive, having first known the ecstasy of going the other way, when at last the body rights itself like one of the cylinders Archimedes trims with Greek letters and tunes in to the laws, and then the slide from stability to veer. You love it when your body rights itself, but lament your wasted years. You love it when your float finally goes under, but you have that exquisite blend of guilt and revel. You are maiming the most beautiful butterfly in the world, making it fly away ragged, doing a mild wing stammer, try-

ing to correct like a doomed pilot whose plane has no trim
tabs, but with the sunlight impartially catching and reveal-
ing its out-of-true wings, the vermilion amid the mauve
that's speckled black. It's perfection that drives us mad:
aspiring to it, and seeing it fail; failing to achieve it, and
thus pretending to aspire to fail. And then not managing to
do even that.

Easier to lower your sights and just get wet. Dip a toe.
Dip a toe for someone else. Damp a hand. Pat water against
the brow. Sit on the ladder and dangle feet. Sit lower on the
ladder, at least a rung down, and wet your bottom. All these
are worthy chores on a torrid summer's day while puffing a
ten-cent cigarillo and joining, *sotto voce*, in the gigantic
ovation of the birds and bees, the grackles and the wasps,
the chipmunks and the dragonflies. You do not have to
swim. You float on an inflatable chair, in one of whose arms
a recess holds a glass of something cold, much as a wooden
leg used to hide a bottle of rum. Strung to your wrist, a pencil helps you to underline anything good in what you read
as you swam around, eyes green-shielded from the sun, un-
dunked skin smeared with sun-block lotion you do not believe in. You really want to burn, with hair on fire. You really want to have an accident, overbalance, and topple
screaming off the float into the deepest water, unable to
breathe for having screamed, but raging to inhale, which
you know you must not do, certainly not while still going
deeper. The book warps at once. The liquid in the glass
blends without demur. The pencil tugs just faintly toward
the surface (which belly dances above you a hundred miles
away), but you drag it down, it goes with you, your eyes
are closed, your heart is going to go off like a grenade until
you turn the page, and it is the sybarite in the book who
drowns, and you smile at his death as you float to and fro,
urged by the tidelet of the inlet valves.

5. MY TUTOR
SHOWS ME HOW

. . . the sea is so near. Next come the oiling-room, the furnace-room, and the antechamber to the bath, and then two rest-rooms, beautifully decorated in a simple style, leading to the heated swimming-pool which is much admired and from which swimmers can see the sea. . . . A dining-room . . . commands the whole expanse of sea and stretch of shore with all its lovely houses. Elsewhere another upper storey contains a room which receives both the rising and setting sun, and a good-sized wine-store and granary behind, while below is a dining-room where nothing is known of a high sea but the sound of breakers, and even that as a dying murmur. . . .

PLINY THE YOUNGER TO GALLUS

Whatever I do in that blue lagoon of mine is somehow not extreme enough. Stroking forward with tongue thrust out to taste and tease the water, I want the chlorine to be fierier, to scald like concentrated peppermint. Swimming naked with an involuntary erection that for the moment has nowhere else to go, I find the contact too fleeting to shove against; its walls are wide and slack and receive you into an ever-newer emptiness you cannot fill. Or, treading away from it toward the inlet valves that pump hot water in, I actually take aim and, in a slow balancing advance, go horning along the runnel of warmth toward the hole in the vinyl wall, determined to push home, but giggle and end up out of reach, my loins pummeled by the long invisible penis of the water, knowing that a successful thrust from me would stump the pump behind the ornamental fence. Mouth wide to receive the liquid raw, although with my breath held tight, I cannot feel its shape, and I know that whatever shape it seems to have is nothing but my mouth's inside. And swimming with eyes closed, while listening to Messiaen's *Quartet for the End of Time* or one of Villa-Lobos's *bachianas brasileiras,* I don't get quite the sense of cosmic exaltation I would like: whereas the same music, hummed underwater, when it is diffused and fumbling, makes my mind quiver and come unstuck, reminding me that this is a world in which, tucked into or enfolded with one another for a while, we babble, howl, roar, and sigh, and then it's over: no more tuck or fold. That's what the underwater music plays, and when the tear comes, in response to the irresistible nastiness of things, you realize that life isn't an alternative to anything at all. Water is the place to leave the tear; where it's least identifiable, least apart.

Something impalpable dismays me. The water always gets away; and whatever I think it expresses, when it clanks or sucks, it doesn't, any more than for me the word *water* is watery or *death* deathlike. In water, you end up with an exaggerated sense of self or an exaggerated notion of nothingness. You doze feathery. You slither at your work. You corrugate your fingertips. You roll about like a blood cell. You mildly annihilate yourself. You call an I a you. That's part of it. And, sometimes, the water changes tune, like the airport announcer who, some distance from the hubbub in the terminal, seems to halt in mid-phrase because the noise got through and then resumes, louder, with a testy intonation. When that happens in the water, and I know it isn't me in the act of imagining, I have an extraordinary sense of new capacity: I am doing something nobody else has dreamed of doing; and, with my back arched like a flying buttress made of toast, I gambol and cavort, the first of my kind: an alga, a sponge, a gymnastic weed. Then everything is possible and nothing goes away; a big warm tide erupts within me, fraught with all the physical harmony I can have, and I not only swim, I go translucent, I become an aqueduct, a creature frail as twirls of light and definite as wire, twisting slowly, as if I've been borrowed by the water, and need neither float nor tread, nor make a stroke, nor call aloud. My ancestors are watching. That I know. Their barely opened lids are mine, and I am the sun eavesdropping on itself, as safe in here as that ordinary yellow star up in the sky.

I can even feel quite pleased, with water and with me, at least until one of Diane's masterly set pieces begins, all of it done in the very top of the water, almost as if she isn't using it at all. First the dive, like a scimitar thrown in some unlikely circus act: a line lancing downward behind the chevron of black hair. No splash to speak of shows me how to do this thing. She skitters along in a speed float and then begins to alternate almighty slaps that make the water foam around her legs. When she speeds up, I hear a rapid surf-like trounce that is the noise of slow and motoric power. Marking time, she marks the water too, which rocks madly up the vinyl sides to get away from her sleek-limbed thrash. Yet she always swims beyond her foam, a jet pilot whose mind flies ahead of the machine. All I can hear is suction, pounding, and a scansion with no pauses in it: *Crushumble-cashumble* it goes, generated by no human form, but the sound of the surface in labor. None of what she does with, and to, the water resembles in the remotest degree my own callow swipes. How weird that, in dominating these thousands of azure gallons, she seems to use so few of them, like someone insulting the law by stealing a policeman's hat. Where she swims is thunder-froth, yet where she doesn't swim seems at her mercy too, especially when she dons black-rubber fins and thwacks the H_2 from its O. Being a purist of some kind, I refuse to use them, wanting to do the thing naturally; but I envy her this white commotion, the black wedge she becomes as she sounds and soars. She seems to ignore the water, as if it had no quality, no image, no being, and then she just as quickly ends the demonstration: out and into a towel while the troubled water jactitates, upset as never by me, and I think of toilets whose cisterns don't refill until you jiggle the lever a dozen times, and the water's oval smooths out, the half-dozen rosettes of turbulence along the rim peel away and vanish until there is only one left, which squirms and bloats before giving up the ghost.

I do not like to swim in the turbid water she has left behind her, so I wait, poring over the text of such magnificently honed piscinery, in which the body writes its will, slams the liquid as if slamming some dumb animal. Not one in a thousand swimmers is ever that good, I know; it has taken her half her lifetime to get this far, to be this javelin, this threshing machine that goes so fast you hardly see

the whirr. She learned to swim before she was old enough
to think about what water was, almost before she had an
identity, before she knew she was separate from anything at
all, like a baby kangaroo homing to its mother's pouch: im-
pelled profoundly, all participant, and not in the least a
spectator. If you miss such primal holism the first time
around, it's hard to find it again, and, even if you succeed,
it's always a little bit willed.

Innocence yields brilliance: That must be it, I decide,
and I vow to dump all the pensiveness of my water-haunted
childhood, then start afresh and become as good at this as
she. Wan hope, it dies the instant I begin to thunder with
my legs, dawdling on my back, and wonder what it would
be like to do it prone. I try it, but my arms miss unison with
my flickering legs, which then lose rhythm altogether, so I
settle for something easier and go swanning about the pool
in a lazy back-paddle, the stroke I reinvented after the rest
of the civilized swimming world had thrown it out. Not for
me the dives known as Swan, Seal, Turtle, Mercury, and
Cannonball, nor the Etonian Plunge, the Cutaway Somersault, the One-and-a-Half Mollberg Somersault, the Isander
(Half Gainer) One-half Twist, which I'm told is perhaps the
most beautiful of the fancy dives, whereas the Hand Stand
with Forward Cut Through and One-half Gainer is one of
the most difficult. With the lingo I am glad to play; I can
relish this chapel's rituals without involving myself in its
most advanced miracles. My breaststroke I will hone, my
funny little topple-dive from the shallow ladder I'll perfect,
my tread I'll get more vertical until it has become what Ber-
nardi in 1794 called "upright swimming," which even has a
moral tone. My swimming will wax and wane, just as it has
throughout the writing of these pages: some days almost
competent, some days no more than a lazy finning float.

Sometimes, when I can't see the pool, I hear the non-stop
suction of her swimming: that aerated pummel, those

thudding aspirates, from which I have learned nothing at all, except how to admire such lightly worn virtuosity, and I know that something perfect is being done, an ode to the water is writing itself longhand, long-leg. Sometimes her rhythm slows, and I savor the lull between one bubble-beaded thwack and the next, knowing that what I hear is the perfect timing of float and push, of kinetic energy almost gone and new energy supplied. Her tail swats the slop away. Pale blue wattles of water fly off and up, changing shape in the sunlight even though a wall is between me and them. The whole pool seethes with her passing, her adroit caroms, her lithe recoveries, and I'm almost glad I cannot see, in the mirror of such excellence, how lousy a swimmer I truly am. It's best to swim my mediocre swims alone, although I no longer know the humiliation of being unable to catch a ball because I need my arms to tread with. A Peruvian friend, in jaunty evocation of Italy—where all kinds of *commendatores* abound—has appointed me *Il Commendatore della Piscina:* a compensatory echo of all the meaningless titles in the world, a bit like putting a blind man in charge of the Louvre. I feel boundlessly tolerated—I the *Commendatore* with the Beginner Swimmer badge—by all the tutors, lifesavers, Peruvians, astronomers, and poets who show their paces in the pool where I deploy my inabilities (although at the same time having, I think, just as much fun). They know not to knock me over or to swim too near while I am trying to get my limbs to work together. Promising throwback that I am, I have loyal friends, who half-believe they'll never see me drown.

I think that, to become flawless at swimming, to become so without also becoming immortal, would sicken me. Silly and sour-grapish as that sounds, I do not want to see too much of any perfection that goes to waste, as bodies do, as poems do not. I would rather stay uncouth, awkward, halting, than achieve an expertness that leaves no record of it-

self. My mortality is what has made me an obstinate amateur, a veteran beginner, though I concede mortality's
what makes us everything we are. In this, though, I go the
other way, choosing imperfection, using a total excuse for a
minor purpose, not having the heart to excel. Not even having perfect swims for the rest of my days would reconcile
me to having to give them up and lose my skill. When I
give it up, it'll be a poorish thing I won't mind letting go,
whereas with some other things I'll part only in indignant,
terminal fury. Over prowess I'll take artifacts, I guess. To a
universe as insecure and ungiving as to want me to pray to
it, currying favor and spouting praise, I will not pray or
even speak. In that little zone I will not serve. I'll take my C
with equanimity, much as someone on the land, or in the
air, long past Reno and the Humboldt Desert, with nothing
much in view, and leaving much to be desired, thinks a
while about Utah, unseen or glimpsed from up on high,
then turns his back on it and doesn't move again.

Yet, having arrived at that point, I change my mind. In a
few cast-off blue books, I begin to write these recollections
of a liquid transit, little realizing that to do so will make
me nervous of deep water all over again. Reliving the
traumas drains the skill from me until, two years later, I
begin almost obliviously twisting about in the top two feet
again. What's below me is just water, more of the same, as
wholesale buyers say. I swim with my mind on other things,
so as not to think about that water underneath. Why is the
music of Edmund Rubbra, to me the symphonic heir of
Ralph Vaughan Williams, so neglected? Like that of Roy
Harris, whom it sometimes evokes. Why do I want to design
and build and fly a model sailplane called *Venerable Bede?*
Who are the oldest waiters in the Hotel Algonquin? Why is
the space telescope taking so long? Is the pinball machine
doomed in an age of video games? Is the public's newborn

passion for fact and how-to books going to oust altogether
the book of subjective witness: the book of how things *feel?*

Even in the center of this continent, I get the same feelings of precariousness, vulnerability, that oceanic sense of
the land, so much so that, during a sustained and highly
agreeable stay in Wichita—a neglected city rather like a
cowboy's idea of Berlin—I began writing poems again,
mainly to get concisely down some images of intimidating
vastness and fragile dependency, couched in the heads of
other tightrope walkers as follows:

> Mothball cowboys pause at intersections
> when the hooded lights say Walk,
> and tilt back upon tall heels, fazed
> by invisible wire, *the edge of things,*
> near which they hunker down, out of the wind,
> behind a concrete block they cannot see
> as the brute foot of a leaping ramp
> to a wholly different range beyond the hewn
> glass of the banks, the bottles in the gutters,
> where jets outcurl their own black smoke:
> bandannas for *g*'s pulled, choking back the *gee*
> which says "We're kind of dizzy where we're at.
> The Atchison, Topeka has become the Santa Fe.
> At midnight on the Chisholm Trail, tornadoes
> march raucous and aloof, while such as we,
> expatriate snowmen, bunkhouse revenants
> who will never ride again, lift up that big lid
> of the blues, and make unsteady campsite here:
> blanket of bacon, bed of beans, a hip-hole
> that will suck us in before the dawn comes up.

Another of these Wichita poems pays incidental tribute to
one of the most charming indoor pools I've seen, but is
mostly an attempt to pin down something phantom and elu-

sive I found in that city, as if at times the life had been
sucked right out of it—maybe that Berlin feeling all over
again.

> Wichitans look through it as if it were
> an era with an aura's half-invisible face,
> and only the chronic stroller finds those arbors,
> troughs, the sunken loveseats invulnerable
> to the wind that shapes a steady wave-front
> from the unkempt river, the unsat-in park
> along its bank: Arkansas or Ur-kansas, said
> with just a touch of plunder in the pride.
> Low down, under bogus parapets, verdigris
> bronze Indians on dead-halt pintos mark
> a racial pause in basins water never fills,
> unless the Holiday Inn be overflowing
> or, from almost as high, sixth wedge in a prism,
> the cobalt indoor pool of the Wichita Royale
> has sprung a leak unstanched by tropic fronds,
> the porous placemats on the Irish linen, navel-
> high above emerald astroturf on deck, and high up
> only girders, an atrium sky that condors
> have dimmed with lime. The city sits up straight,
> awaiting a wallflower lover from the plains.

It felt like that. The something that was bound to happen
remained a guess. It was not the Royale's catching fire when
a First Lady stayed there. It was more like the plains moving in on the city and wiping it out in one glitch, ramming a
gigantic tectonic plate over it for almost ever. And the non-
stop wind felt like a harbinger of that event. As I say, it was
a sense of profound and spacious insecurity (or immaturity,
at that), boiling down to another sense that, not quite
indifferent after all, the universe didn't want me, or any of
us, except to reclaim botched raw material in the interests
of making something new. Akin to my sustained shudder at

winter, it reminded me of an attitude I have never quite outgrown, which says that winter isn't worth spending money on, so buy the cheapest winter clothing possible: a miser of hibernation. So I have a fine collection of ten-dollar overcoats and eighty-cent Korean plastic gloves, whereas on other seasons I am always willing to splurge on a colorful shirt, like a bird reassuming plumage for display. When I really grow up, I suppose I'll buy a really good-quality winter coat instead of making token gestures of aversion (at most) or non-cooperation (at least). The matador of blue water grows up into a pilgrim too, not so much combative, as during all those years of learning, as devout; at any rate, impressed. Yet I will always think, I believe, that you shouldn't offer all of yourself to something that is going to take you anyway. I resent that monopoly of me. I will not give a deliberately helping hand. I will not suck up to it.

How slowly I have learned, not so much to swim, as how to break the habit of assuming a stance and saying there it is, that part of me will never change. It always does. I vow to become no better at swimming, then I improve my breaststroke in a tiny way, using my legs a bit better. I tell myself, with ample reason, that with me swimming has become a kind of cosmic soaring in which I leave behind me things like migraine, gargoyles, nightmares, mishaps, the incessant midnight lamp of the scholarship boy; yet, at times, that isn't true, and I swim because I truly dote on it, and I do so with mind closed, my senses given over wholly to the suck and scurry, the sheer hydraulics. No one else I know swims in the pouring rain, naked save for a hat and a cigar. No one else takes into the water that hand-sized model of the *Widgeon* seaplane, lodges it between the big toe and its neighbor, and lets the plane come cruising up toward him like a test specimen in a wind tunnel full of water. I marvel at the curve of its rise, its final vault to the surface, where it rocks tail down. Who else goes into the water to drink coffee or to read? Or, with a gale howling down from Canada and the first flecks of snow falling, paddles around in a cloud of floodlit steam and chuckles at the bouncing mirage atop the heater's chimney. A lump of childhood has come back, from when I was too scared or too studious to have it, and my local sense of the universe has made of me a permanent water baby.

It is no accident that my "model" of the Milky Way, four feet by one, hanging on its nail in the hallway, shows the Galaxy in white against the bluest blue, with painted thumbtacks for all the different colors of many stars. Here and there, the supermarket paper bag on which I painted it shows through, a mundane touch amid the marvelous. There are many worlds in one, and I am many-minded about them, with a deep sense of having gone through rites of passage—maybe in the wrong order to a lesser destination; but the trip has been worth the fare. I prefer galaxies to planets, I suppose, *if* I have to choose, but I don't know what the swimming equivalent of the preference is. Perhaps I prefer water to swimming in it. Bits of me have yet to grow, like the lily and iris bulbs that Diane embeds in the post-rain earth, like little bon-bombs of bud to feed the eye next spring. Perhaps I prefer fluidity to water itself, flux to dams, and, over and above them all, the thing that contains them all: the sublime *oikos*, the housing of everything, a glimpse of which I sometimes get, from books on galaxies, from hearing friends talk science. A four-hundred-pound gorilla at Stanford University tries to scare people with a small model crocodile! Left-handed methionine has a taste, but its right-handed version doesn't. There is no discernible mathematical reason for the "wobbles" or "degeneracies" in the genetic code, which works so well. I like such stuff. I make my dreams come true in it. I ride that flood.

We live in Porlock, where the universe keeps interrupting us, never mind how useful the thing we're doing. I think I'll write an irritable primer about God, I who in childhood soaked up everything. I go out to examine the water, its level, its heat, its pH factor, but I'm wondering about the etymology of *fastidious* and the origin of the phrase *cut the mustard* and why we pick up not only the receiver but the cradle of the phone too and walk about with it as if we have the lid in one hand and the chalice in the other. The etymology is dubious, but not so much as the dubiology is etymous. My untied shoelaces flap against my ankles. The touch is that of dragonfly wings. We sing "Shenandoah" in the water, agree that you should kill ground insects only with a naked foot. There is nothing that is not interesting. The universe puts up with us, gives us both costly and free samples, and makes the knowable unique. You do not have to travel to find it, but the knowledge of it costs you your life, and then your life becomes part of the knowable that others will have to give their lives to know. All it doesn't do, unlike some London buses, is give you the one reminder: Mind your head when leaving.